OUR NEAREST KINSMAN

OUR NEAREST KINSMAN

The message of redemption and revival in the Book of Ruth

by
ROY
HESSION

CHRISTIAN LITERATURE CRUSADE
Fort Washington, Pennsylvania 19034

CHRISTIAN LITERATURE CRUSADE
Fort Washington, Pennsylvania 19034

CANADA
Box 189, Elgin, Ontario KOG 1EO

© 1976
Christian Literature Crusade, Hampshire, England
First Published 1976
This Impression 1984

ISBN 87508-229-7

All Scripture quotations are from the Authorized (King James)
Version of the Bible, unless otherwise stated. Quotations from
other versions are marked in the footnotes as follows: RV, the
Revised Version of 1881; ASV, the American Standard Version of 1901; and RSV, the Revised Standard Version of 1952,
permission for which latter quotations are by the Division of
Christian Education of the National Council of the Churches
of Christ in the U.S.A.

PRINTED IN U.S.A.

'Spread therefore thy skirt over thine handmaid: for thou art a near kinsman'

—Ruth 3:9.

TO
My dear friends, Ernst and Idi Krebs
in whose hospitable home in Switzerland much of the work
on this book was done.

CONTENTS

PREFACE

I have been led to make a fresh study of the book of Ruth through the gateway of personal need, and that is the gateway through which it is always best to approach the Scriptures. Some time ago I was feeling in a low state spiritually when I heard coming from my record-player the words and music of a chorus which was new to me,

> Cover me, cover me,
> Extend the border of Thy mantle over me,
> Because Thou art my nearest Kinsman,
> Cover me, cover me, cover me.

It was based, of course, on the words of Ruth to Boaz in chapter 3, verse 9, 'Spread thy skirt over thine handmaid, for thou art a near kinsman.' As I listened, my heart was touched. I saw myself a Christian as impoverished as Ruth was, but I saw the Lord Jesus as my nearest Kinsman, my Boaz, who had the right to redeem me out of my new situation of need, and I prayed almost literally the words that Ruth once uttered to Boaz. I confessed my need and asked Him to spread His skirt over His erring servant, that is, to take me on and bail me out again. And He did just that for me that day.

In singing that chorus since then I have seen a special significance in the words, 'extend the border of Thy mantle over me.' I have sometimes found myself so cold in heart that I have wondered if the mantle of grace would stretch as far as me. I need not have feared, for I have found that mantle to be made of wonderfully stretchable material, and that the grace of God by its very nature extends to every conceivable condition of need and culpability. This was how Charles Wesley saw the love of God:

So wide it never passed by one,
Or it had passed by me.

As a consequence of all this, I have looked again at the
book of Ruth from which these words spoke to me. The result
is the heart-moving chapters of this little book. They have
certainly been heart-moving to me, and I can only pray that
they will be so to the reader and they will afford him a new
vision of Jesus as 'our nearest Kinsman.'

As the book of Ruth is one of the lesser-read books of the
Old Testament, I have added at the end an appendix with the
whole text of its four chapters set out as it stands in the
Authorised Version, commonly known as the King James
Version. The text is divided up in such a way as to conform
to the chapter headings of this writing. It is surprising
how even those who regard themselves as having some
familiarity with the book of Ruth have actually only a
superficial knowledge of the story based largely on its senti-
mental aspects, and have missed some of the finer and more
subtle details, which are essential to an understanding of its
message. This was certainly true of me until I began this
present study of the book. I have found it to be an extremely
taut writing, with nothing included which does not mean
something essential to the development of the story, and thus
to its message for us. This means that one cannot afford to
ignore even the smallest phrase, assuming that it has no
significance. I would, therefore, urge the reader to flip over to
the appendix every now and then to refresh his memory as to
the details of the story, and also to consult some more modern
versions if he finds the meaning obscure in any place, not that
I personally have found such in the Authorised Version.

I have also included in the Appendix the text of the two
laws of Moses on which the book of Ruth is based.

London, England, 1976   ROY HESSION

REDEMPTION AND REVIVAL IN THE BOOK OF RUTH

As I have studied this charming book of just four chapters, I have discovered that it is an epic on the great subject of redemption. It is so because the whole story is based on an ancient law of Moses which, in the event of a man having had to sell his family lands because of poverty, gave his next of kin the right to redeem them and restore them to him.[1] In every transaction regarding the sale of land some such clause was clearly understood by everybody. The land was always bought with the proviso that if there was a next of kin who had the means with which to do it, he had the right to redeem for his brother that which he had sold and the purchaser could not say him nay. And this right extended not only to the redemption of land, but also to that of persons. Leviticus 25:47–48 envisages a situation where a man has not only sold his lands, but he has actually sold himself to be the slave of another in order, presumably, to meet his debts. Even when things had come to that pass, it says, 'he may be redeemed again; one of his brethren may redeem him.'

In every fiftieth year, in what was called the year of jubilee, all lands in any case were restored to their original owners and every slave was released and returned to his family.[2] In that great festive year, when with the blowing of trumpets liberty was proclaimed throughout the land, it was decreed, 'ye shall return every man unto his possession and ye shall return every man to his family.' But fifty years was a long time to wait; some might never live to see the next jubilee and thus might never repossess their lands, or be reunited to their families. And so this gracious law of redemp-

---

[1] Lev. 25:23–25 [2] Lev. 25:8–17

tion-rights vested in the next of kin was placed on the
statute book to offer the hope of restoration and release even
before the fiftieth year.

Such a next of kin was given a special name, in Hebrew
goel, which is translated in the book of Ruth 'near kinsman.'
However, elsewhere in the Old Testament it is normally
translated 'redeemer.' So when you read the word redeemer
in the Old Testament, and it is usually spoken of God, you
can take it that in nearly every case it is this word *goel*, with
all these compassionate associations.

More than all this, under the laws of Moses a man had the
duty when his brother died without issue to take on the
widow as his wife and raise up seed to his brother, who would
bear his brother's name and inherit his lands.[1] But for this
provision, family lands first apportioned to each tribe under
Joshua would be lost to that family, and the family itself
would become extinct. This law as set out in Deuteronomy 25
puts this duty only upon the brother of the deceased, but
from the way in which the story of Ruth develops, it seems it
had come to be regarded as the duty of the nearest kinsman,
the *goel*, whether he was as close as a brother or not.

The book of Ruth is based on these two kindly laws of
Moses, and provides the most complete instance in the Bible
of how they worked out in practice – and a beautiful story it is.
The key verse is, I suggest, Ruth 3:9, where Ruth says to
Boaz, 'I am Ruth thine handmaid: spread thy skirt over thine
handmaid; for thou art a near kinsman,' that is, a *goel*. In
asking him to spread his skirt over her in the threshing-floor
that night, she was not guilty of immodesty; it was a symbolic
act whereby she claimed that as a *goel* he would exercise his
right to redeem her family's lost inheritance and take her on
as his wife. Needy, impoverished Ruth made her appeal to
this law of Jehovah and did not find Him, or Boaz, to fail.

Now redemption is the supreme activity of the grace of

[1] Deut. 25:5–10

God, to which all the energies of Father, Son and Holy Spirit are bent. There are two activities of God; the one was creation and the other was and is redemption. The result of the first activity, creation, went all wrong; Satan came in and spoilt it. But God did not despair; He 'made it again another vessel, as seemed good to the Potter to make it' – and that is redemption. To create He had only to speak; but to redeem He had to bleed. And He was willing to do it, though to do so would involve Him in so great a cost. And this was sheer grace on His part. Grace is defined in one dictionary as a 'concession not claimable as a right.' And man had no right to expect to be redeemed. But God did it, and the angels marvelled.

Usually we equate redemption with the forgiveness of sins, according to Ephesians 1:7, where it says 'We have redemption through His blood, the forgiveness of sins.' Thank God, redemption does include that. But if you import into the New Testament word 'redemption' these Old Testament associations on which it is based, you find it is a far bigger thing than that which only deals with the forgiveness of sins. Redemption is that activity of the grace of God that not only forgives a man's sins, but also restores and overrules all the loss occasioned by his sin. And what loss we have subjected ourselves to because of our folly, sin and pride. We lose our experience of blessedness—'Where is the blessedness I knew when first I saw the Lord?' We lose our happy relationships with others, in the home, in the church, in the world outside, and we set people against us. We make mistakes and wrong choices because of self-will, and can find ourselves in grievous and complicated situations as a result. But failure with God is never final. Jesus Christ is the Redeemer of lost men and lost situations, whether the situation has been wrong for half a life-time, or only a day. And when He moves in to redeem, He not only forgives the sin we confess, but He also overrules for good the whole situation in which we have landed ourselves. And when He starts doing that sort of thing, He does it in style. He so often gives back to a man far more than he forfeited, so that he cannot go on blaming himself, but is lost in wonder, love and praise for all that grace has done for a poor failure like himself. Oh, this great and marvellous God of redemption!

The wider meaning I see in this word, redemption, is not unlike the meaning in that other great word beginning with Re, revival. Re is the Latin prefix meaning 'again.' The Bible words beginning with it have a fascination for me, for they always speak of the grace of God—*re*storing, *re*newing, *re*generating, *re*viving. It is God doing something again after man has spoilt it. Finney says that revival is nothing less than a series of new beginnings—God doing something again, and if that goes wrong, doing it yet again.

Redemption and revival, then, are the truths of which the book of Ruth contains a very special picture. As the old serial stories used to say after an introductory paragraph or two, 'and now read on . . .'

CHAPTER 2

NAOMI, THE PRODIGAL DAUGHTER
OF THE OLD TESTAMENT

'I went out full, and the Lord hath brought me home again empty.'

The first chapter of the book of Ruth is a very important one. Every preacher knows, or should know, he has to begin by awakening a sense of need in his hearers. He cannot plunge in too quickly with the positive side of his message. He must first convince the people that they are in just that state of need which requires the provision he proposes to speak about. So it is, before we are introduced to the subject of redemption in the book of Ruth, we have brought before us a story of trouble and loss which occasions the need for one who can redeem. And that is what the first chapter is all about.

Although the title of the book is Ruth, the central character of the first chapter is Naomi, whom I think we can describe as the prodigal daughter of the Old Testament. As we pursue the story we cannot but notice certain marks of similarity between her and the prodigal son in our Lord's parable in the New Testament. That son, as he returned, could well have used the same words that Naomi did, 'I went out full, and the Lord hath brought me home again empty.' True, he did not remain empty and neither did Naomi; and that is what the remaining chapters of the book of Ruth unfold.

We are introduced to a happy Israelite family. The father's name was Elimelech, which is Hebrew for 'God is king.' They lived in a little town called Bethlehem, which means 'the house of bread,' and it was doubtless so called because it aptly described its condition. It was set in a rural area where the fields were wonderfully fertile and they lacked nothing. His wife's name was Naomi, which in Hebrew means 'pleasant,' and it was fitting that this should be her name in such a situation. They had two sons, named Mahlon and

Chilion. Hebrew scholars seem to differ on the meaning of these two names, so I select that view which accords most with the message I want to bring out. Mahlon, according to one book of reference means 'song,' and Chilion means 'complete.' If we take these names as descriptive in some sense of their condition, what a family we have here! God was their king, they lived in a house of bread, theirs was a pleasant experience of life, song often filled their lips and with it a sense of completeness.

Whether you think this fanciful or not, it certainly provides us with a picture of what life in Christ is meant to be. If we have come to know the Lord Jesus, God is intended to be our king, ruling us in all things. And when He does so, we find ourselves living in a house of bread, for Jesus said, 'he that cometh to me shall never hunger; and he that believeth on me shall never thirst,'[1] and that means real satisfaction. In such a case our experience can be called pleasant, for of Wisdom it is said, 'Her ways are ways of pleasantness, and all her paths are peace.'[2] It does not mean that our situations will always be easy, but on the inside we may have peace and be happy. Ours is to be the Mahlon experience of songs of praises to Him Who is meeting our needs, and the Chilion experience of life in Christ being complete and fulfilling. That is God's intention for the life where He is allowed to rule as king.

But here in this story we are told there came a day when there was a famine in the land and especially in Bethlehem-Judah. The rains, it would seem, had ceased to come at their usual seasons, and that probably not for one year, but for several years. As a result, crops had failed and there was a terrible famine in the area. Could it be, famine in the 'house of bread'? Surely not; but so it was. It was the very opposite of what one would have expected, a virtual denial of the very name of Bethlehem. Had God not also said about the Promised Land that it was to be a land of milk and honey, where His people would eat bread without scarceness?

[1] John 6:35   [2] Prov. 3:17

Indeed, He had; but He had also said in various places that if His people who were called by His name should turn away from Him, worshipping other gods, transgressing His laws, and not be willing to repent, He might well find it necessary to shut up heaven that there should be no rain, and even to command the locusts to devour the land and, further, to send pestilence among His people.[1]

Sadly, this too is pictorial of what sometimes happens in the life of a Christian. Yes, it is a land of milk and honey for him, but if he turns away from the Lord his God in this matter or that, and will not heed the word of correction that God is sure to give him, He sometimes finds it necessary for the restoration of that saint to shut up heaven over his head that there be no rain. The refreshing movings of the Spirit are no longer known in his heart, the Bible becomes dead, prayer is empty, personal witness and Christian service are chores and he ceases to have a joyous testimony. What a terrible possibility that there can be such a famine in our souls! Amos talks about a famine, not 'of bread, nor a thirst for water, but of hearing the words of the Lord.'[2] That is a famine indeed when we cease to hear from heaven, and who of us has not known such times? And all this can take place, if you please, in the 'house of bread.'

But God had also said that if His people who were called by His Name, finding themselves in such a situation, would humble themselves and pray, and seek His face and turn from their wicked ways, then He would hear from heaven, and would forgive their sin, and would heal their land. And this is what Elimelech should have done when he found himself in the midst of this famine. Doubtless he was a leading man in the town and he should have stayed where he was and led the people in days of humbling and prayer before God. He should have been one of those who sought the face of God to know for what cause He had shut up heaven, and put right what God showed was wrong. Had he done so, there is no

[1] 2 Chron. 7:13–14   [2] Amos 8:11

doubt but that God would have been gracious and would have heard from heaven and healed the land. But he did not do it; instead he found another way out. The land of Moab, the Gentile heathen country next door, did not seem to have any famine; their fields were green and fertile. So instead of staying where he was and getting right with God together with others, he gathered his little family together and made off to that other country, being quite sure he would do better for himself there. In doing so he left his precious lands, which had been in his family ever since they were apportioned in the days of Joshua. It is not clear from the narrative whether he actually sold them at this time; probably not, because we are told he only went to 'sojourn.' Doubtless he told his friends, 'I'm only going for a short time, just to sojourn; I'll be back soon.' It was a long sojourn; he never did come back, nor did his sons; and when at last Naomi did, ten long years had passed, during which time the family farm had lain untended and gone back to long grass, with the family home itself falling into complete disuse.

Now this is just what we do. When we are in a time of famine, rather than seek the face of the Lord as to why we are in this state, so cold in heart and out of touch with God, we look at other fields, the fields of the world, and set our hearts on them. I use the word 'world', in the sense that the Apostle John uses it when he says 'Love not the world,'[1] meaning, of course, not the physical world of nature, but human society organised apart from God; and friendship with that world, whether it is ostensibly bad or not, is enmity with God.[2] And here is the reason why some Christians go back into it, in larger or smaller degrees—not because the world is so attractive, but that Bethlehem has become so dry. Jesus is not real any more. They feel they must have some bit of fun in life, some bit of joy, something to occupy their time. It appears to them that there is now nothing among the saints to attract them, for everything there seems dead. But whose

[1] 1 John 2:15   [2] James 4:4

fault is that? Could it be that it is you who is dead and dry, not the saints? Whose fault is it that He Who is their joy has become so dull to you, that your heart is now set on the fields of Moab? Of course, it is your fault, our fault. But instead of facing it out and getting back to the source of joy, we go like the prodigal son did, and like Naomi did, into a far country to find some substitute there for what we have lost.

And in doing all this we forsake our precious inheritance of joy and liberty in Jesus Christ. As the old Gospel hymn says,

> And never from thy Lord depart,
> With Him of every good possessed.

But we have done just that; we have departed from the One with whom we were possessed of every good, and have only got ourselves involved in a whole range of new problems. Meantime our inheritance in Christ remains untended, un-enjoyed. We tell ourselves that these excursions into the fields of Moab are only going to be for a short time, just a sojourn, just a little outing, just a little lowering of the standards of our consecration to God, in order to enjoy what the world has to offer. But, you know, that short time is not always such a short time. There you may be to this day, having forsaken the enjoyment of your once-fruitful fields.

GOD'S HAND OF DISCIPLINE

If we remain in the far country, it is certainly not for lack of God taking means to bring us back. For Naomi had not been many years in the land of Moab before God began to work to lead her back, such was His love for her. Naomi is now the object of our attention, rather than Elimelech, and our whole interest from this point is on her return. That she did return was only because God used two things to cause her to repent of the family's ill-considered decision in the first place. First, He laid His hand of discipline upon her family and she lost her husband, Elimelech. Grievous as this blow was, she felt she still had bread-winners in the persons of her two sons—until God took them also. There she was bereft indeed, left of her husband, left of her two sons, alone in the world in a country to which she did not belong, with two Moabite daughters-in-law with whom she had no blood tie, or racial link other than the fact that they had married her sons. God had caused life in that land to become bitter indeed for her. She herself put it this way, 'Call me not Naomi (which means pleasant), call me Mara (which means bitter), for the Almighty hath dealt very bitterly with me.'

The love of God for us is such that no sooner do we get away from Him, than He works to bring us back. And what He uses to bring us back is very often His discipline, the losses He allows to come upon us. First of all, Elimelech dies, that is, God ceases to be king in our lives. That is a loss indeed, though at first we do not seem to mind, we prefer to go our own way rather than His. But then we find Mahlon and Chilion die—we lose our song and all sense of fulfillment in life, and we are left with only a faint memory of days when we used to rejoice. Then, sometimes, He takes a more direct hand in our affairs to ensure that we realise He is dealing with us, and He allows us to come into all sorts of grave and difficult situations, and we become embittered Christians.

However, let me say emphatically that these experiences are not to be regarded as punishments. They are always and all the time restorative in their intention, rather than punitive. Whatever a man may suffer, no matter how grievous or calamitous, it is never to be regarded as a punishment for sin, for the simple reason it can never be severe enough to be so regarded. The only adequate punishment for sin is what Jesus bore in His body on the tree for us. There and there only do we see the due reward for our sin. No, what comes to us is designed to bring us back to the God who loves us, by provoking us to repent of our wrong choices and by making the far country less attractive for us to remain there. As William Cowper says in his famous hymn,

> Behind a frowning providence,
> He hides a smiling face.

It is all the love of God working for our restoration.

I must pause here to amplify and qualify all this lest we might still misinterpret God's dealings with us. I say, still misinterpret, because that is the natural thing for all of us to do. A guilty conscience always makes a man feel God is against him and that anything adverse that happens to him is some sort of a punishment. That is just not so. We must really take seriously that word, 'God was in Christ reconciling the world unto himself, *not imputing unto them their trespasses.*'[1] Especially note that last phrase. Whatever this or that adversity means, it cannot mean that He is imputing unto us our trespasses, because He has already imputed them to Jesus Christ on the cross. 'In all their adversity he was no adversary.'[2] It is simply the love of God intent on restoring us.

It is for this reason that I have avoided using the word 'chasten,' which is the one used in Hebrews 12, because in spite of all that one might say, the idea of punishment still persists in our minds when that word is used. I have rather used the word discipline, but here too our fearing hearts still think of possible reasons of guilt. But the words discipline and disciple simply mean being taught. So when we are in times of spiritual or material adversity, we should not ask why should this be happening to us, but rather, what is God teaching us through it? And we shall find it is invariably with regard to areas where we need to be restored, but to which we have possibly been blind.

This may help those who have been walking as obediently to God as they know how and can hardly be said to have got into any land of Moab, and yet God seems to be nonetheless testing them. I would still say that such trials are restorative in their intention. None of us realises how much was lost in

[1] 2 Cor. 5:19   [2] Isa. 63:9 RV (margin)

the fall of Adam, nor how far the Divine image has been defaced in us. None of us fully realises how extensive is the reign of self. God, however, does realise it, and He is engaged on an unrelenting recovery operation in all of us, an operation that is not the work of one day. It began with our experience of new birth and it will continue for the rest of our lives. Always He will be working to restore us to Himself in new areas where self has known little or no surrender. And trials and losses are designed, if for no more, to give us the opportunity for such surrender.

This surrender of self is not made necessary merely because of the Fall. It was the order of the day even before the Fall. Someone has said, 'An experience of the cross is when God's will crosses ours and we submit to God's.' Even before sin came in, Adam was called upon to walk that way. It is conceivable that God might often have asked Adam to do something that would cross his natural wishes for himself— for instance, to rise and do some task when every fibre of his body was bidding him to rest and sleep. The whole essence of the unfallen relationship to God was that there was no self-adherence in Adam, that in such a case he would immediately and gladly surrender what he wanted to do in order to do God's will, and only be thankful to have the opportunity to make such surrender for the One he loved. When man fell, it simply meant that he refused to do this and he thereby acquired for himself a constitutional tendency to go on refusing. The result was that anything inconvenient he was asked to do, or any apparently adverse thing that Providence allowed to happen was resisted and resented and not embraced as God's will. And, alas, all his descendants have inherited the same constitutional tendency to self-centredness (Paul in his writings calls it 'the flesh'), and they act and react in the same way as their father did.

Trials and losses therefore are not only designed to provoke Naomis to repent of where they have got into the land of Moab, but also to give even the most obedient servant of God the opportunity to surrender to Him his natural desires for himself, and thus know more of that relationship to God where, to repeat, self-surrender has always been the order of the day. I say, the most obedient servant of God, but how immediately obedient are any of us? As sons of fallen Adam, our surrender to God on a new matter invariably has to begin with the confession that out first reaction was not to surrender—nor were possibly our second and third reactions.

GOOD NEWS FROM HOME

We must now return from that important digression to the story before us.

God used a second thing to bring Naomi back to Bethlehem; it was the news of revival back home. 'She had heard in the country of Moab that the Lord had visited His people in giving them bread.' The news came through that the famine had been lifted; the rains had come, the fields were full of grain again and the people were rejoicing. What a picture of revival! It could only mean that some folks back home had been repenting. Maybe a prophet or two had been speaking to them in the Name of the Lord as to what had been wrong and the people had responded; and God had been gracious and healed their land. Such news coming to Naomi in her poverty and misery were obviously calculated to turn her feet back home. It was so with the prodigal son in the New Testament. It was the thought that in his father's house even the servants had bread enough and to spare which was the main factor in turning his face towards home again.

Perhaps Naomi and Elimelech were right in saying that things were so dry in Bethlehem; perhaps you too are right to have said the same about the saints. But God grant that you will hear news in your land of Moab that things are no longer dry among them, that God has been moving in revival there, that some of them have been repenting and seeing Jesus again and that there is a renewal of love amongst them; in a word, that God has visited His people in giving them bread. Sometimes a modern-day Naomi will meet a Christian who is altogether radiant and who seeks to share his joy with her in her misery. That Christian will doubtless hasten to add, 'but it has not been always so with me; up till recently there has been such a famine in my soul and I have been in the midst of a situation of misery too. But God has helped me to go to the cross again, and now all things have become new.' Such a testimony cannot but have a strange effect on the one who hears it and she begins to say, 'if God can do that for him, he can do something for me.' And another Naomi is wanting to start on her way back home.

For Naomi it was not a matter of merely taking to the road again as if there had been nothing wrong in what she had done. Under the influences of God's discipline and news of revival back home, Naomi really repented of ever having left Bethlehem in the first place. The fact that she did so repent is clear from the way in which she spoke at this point. In one place in this chapter she says, 'the hand of the Lord has gone out against me;' in another, 'the Almighty hath dealt very bitterly with me;' and in another, 'the Lord hath testified against me, and the Almighty hath afflicted me.' There is no spirit of complaining about these words, just a gracious, humble recognition that she had been suffering under the hand of God and that she had learnt her lesson.

The way of repentance is the way back to God and to blessing for us too. It is not merely trying to pick up the threads again where we had dropped them; that could be to side-step repentance. Repentance is our justifying of God; it is to recognise that we have been suffering under His hand, that He has been right so to afflict us, and we have no complaints. It is the acknowledgment that in those matters to which He points, He is right and we are wrong. And it is doing all this at the foot of the cross, where the Just died for the unjust to bring us to God. There we can afford to be the wrong ones, for

'Mercy there is great and grace is free,
  Pardon there is multiplied to me,
There my burdened soul finds liberty,
  At Calvary.'

SHE RETURNS TO NOTHING

Now here we come to what I see to be the main point of
this first chapter of Ruth and which relates it to the chapters
that follow. Naomi came back to nothing. She herself said, 'I
went out full and the Lord hath brought me home again
empty.' She went out doubtless with some money, she came
back with none. She went out with her husband and two sons,
she came back without them. When she got back she found
that her contemporaries still had their husbands and sons
with them and were surrounded with grandchildren. But
Naomi came back with none of this; her bright hopes for the
future lay buried in Moab. All she came back with was a
Gentile daughter-in-law, of whose reception by her people
she was far from sure. Above all, she came back to a situation
where she was without land.

Now I thought at my first reading that Elimelech must
have sold his family lands when he first left Bethlehem,
because this is the story of how they were redeemed. The
discussion in the gate of Bethlehem recorded in chapter 4 is
all concerning who is going to redeem Naomi's land, Boaz or
another relative, and the use of the very word 'redeem'
implies that it had been sold. But in verse 3, Boaz says,
'Naomi, that is come again out of the country of Moab, selleth
a parcel of land, which was our brother Elimelech's.' One can
only assume, therefore, that this land had not actually been
sold before they went; it was still there, but neglected and
overgrown for ten years, with the old farmhouse broken
down. She came back with no men-folk to work the farm.
Quite obviously, one of the first things she would have to do
was to sell her land to the highest bidder. Indeed, we can
regard that land as already virtually sold and therefore the

use of the word 'redeem' with regard to it was not inappropriate. And to sell family lands was to sell what every Hebrew family considered its most precious possession. The one thing every family would want to do was to secure their lands for future generations. In this case, however, there was not likely to be any future generation in the name of Elimelech, as her daughter-in-law was a childless widow. The land would thus go out of the family and the family name become extinct. If ever there were candidates for the provisions of redemption in Israel, they were Naomi and Ruth, though at first it seems they were hardly aware of such possibilities.

Now this is exactly our situation. When we come back to God, we come back with nothing, and, it would seem, to nothing. We too, have to say, 'I went out full, and the Lord hath brought me home again empty,' so empty that there is nothing we can do to regain our lost inheritance.

This is precisely the position envisaged in the oft-quoted verse, Matthew 16:26, 'What is a man profited, if he shall gain the whole world, and lose his own soul? Or what shall a man give in exchange for his soul?' This is so well known that we may have missed at least part of its meaning. There are two questions here. First, what is a man profited if to gain what the world has to offer he loses his own soul, that is, he parts with his relationship to God. And the implied answer is, he is not profited at all, he is an utter loser. Then there is a further question; having done that, what can he now give to get it back, to undo the transaction? And the implied answer is quite obviously, he can do nothing; what has been done cannot be undone. Could his zeal no respite know, could his tears for ever flow, there is nothing now that he can do to atone for the sin that he has committed and to recover what he has so wantonly and cheaply sold. In other words, the effects of sin and folly in our lives are irrecoverable apart from the grace of God. Having stained ourselves with guilt, what can we do to regain peace? Having messed up things, what can we do to get them straight again? And the answer, if only we will face it, is that we can do nothing. We have limitless power to commit sin (what giants we are in that realm, if we choose to be!), but we have no power at all to atone for it or undo its effects on ourselves and on our situation once it is done. We sometimes think if we can become better Christians and be nicer to our fellows, that that will restore things. But, for myself, I find the moment I feel I have got to become a little bit better to qualify, I am defeated before I start, for I know from experience that it is becoming that little bit better that always defeats me. And yet we may come back, but like Naomi and Ruth, we come back empty. Bill Gaither expresses it this way in one of his Gospel songs:

If there ever were dreams that were lofty and noble,
  Those were my dreams at the start;
And the hopes for life's best were the hopes that I harboured
  Deep down in my heart;
But my dreams turned to ashes, my castles all crumbled,
  My fortune turned to loss;
So I wrapped it all in the rags of my life,
  And I laid it at the cross.

But be encouraged; though Ruth and Naomi returned empty, they did not remain empty. That is what the story is all about, how the empty became full. And it was all because there back home was one who was their nearest kinsman. And you, too, are not going to remain empty. In coming back to God as an empty sinner saying, 'I'm all wrong, I'm the one to blame,' you become a candidate for the gracious provision of One Who has the right to redeem everything, your nearest Kinsman.

RUTH THE CONVERT

There is one important matter in which Naomi, the prodigal daughter of the Old Testament, differed from her counterpart in the New Testament—when she came back from the far country, she brought another with her. All too often when men go away from God they take others with them; but it sometimes happens that when they repent and come back to the Lord, others are induced to do the same and come back with them. This was certainly true in the case of Naomi. She brought Ruth with her, not merely as one who wanted to be a naturalised Hebrew, but as a convert; for Ruth not only said, 'thy people shall be my people' but also, more important, 'thy God shall be my God.' What is that if it is not an Old Testament conversion?

Now this choice of Ruth's was quite extraordinary because all she had known of Naomi's God was Him, who it would seem, had caused all her troubles to come upon her. This was not much to attract a Gentile girl to Him. Perhaps it was this thought that lay behind Naomi's words when she said, 'It grieveth me much for your sakes that the hand of the Lord has gone out against me." Perhaps she had been hoping for the conversion of her two daughters-in-law and had been wanting them to see how good and beneficent the rule of Jehovah was, that they might choose Him too. But now she feared that all that they had seen happen (and they had suffered too in the process, having lost husbands) would put them off for ever. But it had no such effect on Ruth. In spite of everything she said, 'thy God shall be my God.'

Whatever was it that induced her to make such a choice? I suggest it was the sight of Naomi repenting before her God and, I imagine, gaining peace of heart as she did so. And as she listened and looked the shadow of Jehovah fell across the scene and she saw that He was merciful and gracious to sinners. For, surely, if a person repents before the Lord it implies that there is forgiveness and restoration with Him; why otherwise repent? In a court of law no prisoner as a rule repents (I have been on a jury and I know), for the simple reason there would be nothing gained; justice must take its course whatever the prisoner confesses. Therefore the prisoner usually remains tight-lipped and defensive. If, however, there were a court set up to dispense mercy for self-confessed criminals rather than justice, there would be every inducement for them to make confessions and there might well be a rush of them. And as Ruth saw her mother-in-law taking a sinner's place before God and heard her making confession to Him, she began to realise the implications of it all, that Naomi's God, the One she called Jehovah, was merciful and gracious to sinners. It was because Naomi knew Him to be such that she was humbling herself before Him at all. This was a revelation of His character unique to Israel, ever since that day in the mount when God had proclaimed His Name to Moses, 'Jehovah, a God full of compassion and gracious, slow to anger and plenteous in mercy . . . forgiving iniquity, transgression and sin.'[1]

Perhaps up to that moment Ruth had always thought of Naomi's God as the good person's God, for Naomi had always seemed so good and faultless; and as Ruth knew that she herself was not like that, she felt she could not qualify for such a God. But the day she saw her mother-in-law repenting as a sinner before Jehovah she began to see that He was the sinner's God, One Who delighted in mercy for people who had been wrong; and then it was she said, 'This God shall be my God, for as a sinner myself I qualify.'

This, I suggest is what lay behind the choice that Ruth made; does it commend itself to you? In any case there is something here for us Christians. We want the world to see Jesus in us and we think the way is for them to see an impeccable Christian life. But the only effect of the attempt to do this is so often to give the impression that ours is the good person's God, for we appear to be so good ourselves. This does not draw sinners, but rather discourages them because they feel they are not good enough to qualify. In actual fact, we are not impeccable Christians at all; we are just allowing people to see selected portions of our lives; other parts of our lives would tell a different story. But when they see us repenting and putting things right, when they hear us giving a sinner's testimony and sharing what the Lord is doing for us, then it dawns on them that ours is not the good

[1] Ex. 34:6–7 ASV

person's God at all, but the sinner's God and therefore they can have Him too. In the hushed silence that sometimes follows a costly act of repentance there falls across the scene the shadow of the Saviour of sinners, and others feel drawn to Him as never before. We shall be far more helpful to others by being broken (that is, by taking the sinner's place) than preaching to them as from a pedestal. And as we come back to the cross ourselves, we shall maybe bring with us some precious Ruth, the child of our tears and of our repentance, to find the same peace as we have. Let us be sure, then, that the testimony we give to others is the sinner's testimony; so shall they see the God of grace.

And thus it was Naomi and Ruth came back to Bethlehem together—both of them empty, it is true, but they were not to remain empty, as we shall see.

CHAPTER 3

BOAZ, THE NEAR KINSMAN

'The man is near of kin to us, one that hath the right to redeem.'

Now we come to Boaz, whom I am quite sure the Holy Spirit intends us to see as a type and foreshadowing of the Lord Jesus Christ. The more I wait on God over these Scriptures, the more sure I am that it is no preacher's licence thus to view Boaz and the position he occupies. It is simply another instance of that strange phenomenon with which the Old Testament Scriptures abound, of foreshadowings of the Saviour Who was to come. None of us could be more daring in appropriating Old Testament Scriptures and applying them to Christ than were the writers of the New Testament. We are, therefore, encouraged by their example to look for Christ here.

'Now Naomi had a kinsman of her husband, a mighty man of wealth, of the family of Elimelech, and his name was Boaz.' Naomi, the poorest person in Israel, had for her kinsman one of the wealthiest men in the land, though at first she saw no connection between that fact and her great need. But as we have seen, the next of kin had, according to the law of Moses, both a right and a responsibility with regard to an impoverished relative. According to Leviticus 25, he had the right to redeem for his brother any of his estate which he had lost; and according to Deuteronomy 25, he had the responsibility, where his brother had died without issue, to take his widow as his wife in order to raise up seed in his brother's name to inherit his brother's lands. Such a one was known in the Hebrew as a *goel* to his needy relatives, as we have seen. This then was the position of Boaz, though he had not seen himself as such with regard to Naomi and Ruth. On their part they had not seen him as a *goel* either.

Surely it is impossible to escape the conclusion that we are intended to see in that *goel* of old a foreshadowing of the Lord Jesus, Who by 'countless acts of pardoning grace' down the centuries has shown Himself the Redeemer of lost sinners and the Restorer of hopeless situations. He is neither shocked nor shaken by human sin and the confusion it has caused. Indeed, when He is allowed to take over, He is at His best in such situations, knowing He is the *goel* for all such people, well able to redeem them and their circumstances with the most glorious results. He is a specialist in dealing with sin, and His fame is in the glorious recoveries He accomplishes in that realm.

Here we come to the very heart of the Bible teaching on redemption. It is based on this law of the *goel*, the right to redeem given to the next of kin. Redemption, therefore, is an Old Testament word before it is a New Testament word. And the New Testament truth is based on, and developed from, what we are now considering. It is the fact that the book of Ruth so fully exemplifies this law that confers on it its special importance.

THE RIGHT TO REDEEM

For one man to redeem another, that is to play the part of a *goel*, three things were necessary. First, he had to be a near kinsman—none else had the right to insist that the purchaser sell the land back. Although in the book of Ruth the Hebrew word for kinsman in most places is *goel*, it is not so in every place. In three places words are used which simply mean an ordinary family relation, with no thought of redemption. In the verse where Boaz is first introduced into the story, 'Naomi had a kinsman of her husband's,' the word used is not *goel*, but *moda*. The same word is used in chapter 3, verse 2, 'And now is not Boaz one of our kindred,' that is, is not Boaz our *moda*, our relative linked to us by family ties? The third place is in chapter 3, verse 20, where Naomi says, 'the man is near of kin to us.' Here the word is *qarob*, which means virtually the same as *moda*, a near relative. We can put it this way, that if a man was to be a *goel* to another he had to be a *moda* first.

In the same way, if the Lord Jesus is to redeem on behalf of sinners and failing saints what they have lost, He must acquire the right to do so by becoming their Kinsman, their Brother. This is precisely what happened when the eternal Word was made flesh and dwelt among us. This is the whole meaning of the important passage, Hebrews 2:10–18, where Jesus calls us brethren, and where to qualify Himself to do so He partakes of our humanity. 'Forasmuch, then, as the children are partakers of flesh and blood, He also Himself likewise took part of the same.' I believe that there is a very definite allusion here to the law of the *goel*, because the reason given for His taking part of our flesh and blood and thus becoming our Brother is in close keeping, spiritually speaking, with the work of a *goel*—'that through death He might destroy him that had the power of death, that is, the devil; and deliver them who through fear of death were all their lifetime subject to bondage.' And so it was, 'in all things it behoved him to be made like unto his brethren.' There is no sorrow or trial that our flesh is heir to, but Jesus has been Himself a partaker of it all. I believe it could be shown—and it would be a most interesting study—that there is no loss, or indignity, or deprivation of rights that men suffer, but that Jesus suffered all that and more in the days of His humiliation. The Word says that in *all* things He was made like unto His brethren, and all means all. For this reason, this epistle tells us, He is a merciful and faithful High Priest for us, touched with the feeling of our infirmities, bearing gently with the ignorant and with them that are out of the way.

I am a lover of biography and history and I was once touched to read an incident regarding the death of Princess Elizabeth, a daughter of King Charles I, who was beheaded in Whitehall, London. She was cast into prison, where she

contracted tuberculosis and where she died, sad and neglected. When they found her, her Bible was open, her head lying
on the text, 'Come unto me, all ye that labour and are heavy
laden, and I will give you rest.' The historian at this point
added a little sentence that moved me very much; 'She found
comfort in the One Who as her Brother was made like unto
her in all things.' Yes, Jesus really is our near Kinsman.

However, the Incarnation, which indeed made Him our
near Kinsman, has not made Him near enough, if He is to
redeem us from all our troubles and losses. And that for the
reason that some of these losses and troubles, together with
our spiritual lacks, are due to our own fault and there are
matters in which we are indeed to be blamed. The Incarnation in itself has no answer to culpability, that is, to sin. And
so it was that in order to acquire the right to redeem for us,
the One who had partaken of our flesh and blood had to carry
a cross up to the hill called Calvary and die upon it, there
accepting our culpability as His own and dying our death. At
the manger the Eternal One was 'made in the likeness of
men,'[1] but at the cross He was made 'in the likeness of sinful
flesh'[2] and exhausted God's judgement for us. This means
that by His blood He forgives and cleanses the sins that have
caused the situations. In so doing, He takes the blame out of
sin for sinners, which is just what draws them to Him. In
other words, the cross makes Him the sinner's *nearest*
Kinsman.

A criminal in prison for some shameful crime might well
say to us, 'You talk to me about Jesus being made like us in all
things; but I don't think He has suffered what I suffer—the
shame and disgrace of having done what I have done.' You are
wrong, man; that is just what he has suffered. The shame and
disgrace of sin is precisely what He did experience on the
cross—only it was your shame and disgrace, not His own,
and that must have made it all the harder for Him to bear. As
a result you and every other sinner in the world can look up

[1] Phil. 2:7   [2] Rom. 8:3

to Jesus and say, 'You are my nearest Kinsman, and as such You have the right to redeem me and my situation.'

It must have been a wonderful moment for Naomi when she realised that the one she had always known merely as a relation was by that very fact her *goel*, one of those that had the right to redeem for her. It is a wonderful thing for us too when we have it revealed to us that, in the midst of situations for which we can only blame ourselves, Jesus is our nearest Kinsman, not only our *moda* but our *goel*, that He has the right to redeem all we have lost and that Calvary has given Him that right.

THE POWER TO REDEEM

The second thing that was necessary was that the next of kin should have the power to redeem, that is, the financial means to do so. It was one thing for him to have the right to redeem, but another to have the power to do so. A *goel* would be of little help if he was as poor as the one who needed him. This was not the case with Boaz; he was one of the big farmers in the area and 'a mighty man of wealth.' He not only had the right to redeem, but also the power to do so.

We have seen that the Lord Jesus has acquired the right to redeem and that His blood secures forgiveness and cleansing of our sin in our situations, but has He the power to redeem those situations themselves? He has power on earth to forgive sin, but has He power on earth to make good the results of our sin, the crippling sense of shame to begin with, then the forefeited happiness, the broken relationships with others, the situations of pain and loss? Here faith falters, when it sees all that is involved and when the Devil continually tells us there is no hope of things ever being the same again. We can believe in Christ for the forgiveness of our sins, but we have grave doubts sometimes about what He can do as to their results. Here He challenges head-on our doubts as to His power in this realm, even as Jehovah had to challenge Israel's doubts in Isaiah 50:2, 'Is My hand shortened at all, that it cannot redeem? Or have I no power to deliver?' It was sad that Israel had gone into captivity because of their sin, but it was sadder when, having got there, they did not see that Jehovah was their Kinsman, their *goel*, and believe that His hand yet had power to redeem them from their desolations. So it is we have these wonderfully positive prophecies in Isaiah, Jeremiah and the other prophets, telling the people of the glorious restoration that one day would be theirs, and assuring them that Jehovah was their Redeemer, their *goel* and that, to quote, 'Their Redeemer is strong; He shall throughly plead their cause.'[1] Indeed, the redemption from Babylon is prophesied even before they had gone there, and that in the most glowing terms! The restoration of the ruined city and temple is foretold even before they had become ruins! Such is the extent to which grace antedated sin in Israel's case! What an affecting thing it must have been for them to learn that Jehovah, against Whom they had sinned and under Whose hand they had suffered so many disciplines was nonetheless their nearest Kinsman, intent on their ultimate redemption from it all!

In like manner with us, grace has antedated sin and our nearest Kinsman is 'the Lamb slain from the foundation of the world,' God having anticipated in Him our situations of loss, even before they had arisen. Therefore the might of His right hand is well able to make all things new. The simple fact is that the realm of redeeming what man has lost is the realm where Jesus excels. As we have said before, it is here that He is at His best. He is the divine Potter Who does not despair when He finds the vessel marred in His hands, but makes it again another vessel as seems good to the Potter to make it. And it is wonderful to behold the beautiful new vessel He ultimately makes out of the disfigured mess we present Him with.

[1] Jer. 50:34

Jesus can solve every problem,
  The tangles of life can undo;
There is nothing too hard for Jesus,
  There is nothing that He cannot do.*

These words are true indeed, but with one proviso—that the one in the midst of the problem repents and admits that he himself is the real problem and that he has caused or contributed to the other problems. When he does that, his sin in the matter is utterly forgiven and the mess he has caused is no longer his responsibility but the Lord's, and he can rest it in His hands. It then becomes His raw material from which He shows His power to make a new thing.

Something beautiful, something good,
  All my confusion He understood;
All I had to offer Him was brokenness and strife,
  But He made something beautiful of my life.†

If He is not able to do this, what sort of a Saviour have we?

THE WILLINGNESS TO REDEEM

A third thing was necessary for a *goel*, for one who was to redeem for another. He needed not only to have the right to redeem because he was near of kin, nor only the power to do so, but he had also to have the willingness. A *goel* might not be willing to do it. It was so in the case of the nearer kinsman mentioned in chapter 4. There was one who had a closer kinship to the family of Elimelech than Boaz and who therefore had a prior claim to do this task. At first he was quite willing to redeem the land, but when he learnt it would also mean taking Ruth to be his wife to raise up seed to Mahlon, he backed off. He was not at all sure he wanted to take on this alien girl; he probably already had a wife and two women were more than he could contemplate! He had the right and he had the power, but he had not the willingness. Not so Boaz; he was more than willing. The fact that to make Ruth

* By The Rodaheaver Company. Used by permission.
† By Bill and Gloria Gaither. Used by permission.

his wife was part of the package deal was its chief attraction to him. It is quite clear from the story that he ultimately lost his heart to this Gentile girl whom he first met as a gleaner in his fields.

And the Lord Jesus has not only the right and the power to redeem for you, but also the willingness. He is more than willing for much the same reason that Boaz was willing, for He has lost his heart to you. He is not only concerned in restoring what you have forfeited, in solving your problems and making you happy again, but in having you. That is what makes the whole package deal of redemption so attractive to Him—it means possessing you. When He takes on your lost situation, He takes on you also. He 'gave himself for us, that he might redeem us . . . unto himself a people for his own possession.'[1] Can you believe it? You have so touched His heart, that you are the great attraction to Him? And the fact that you are so loved and desired surely draws you to Him and encourages you to pray,

> Extend the border of Thy mantle over me,
> Because Thou art my nearest Kinsman,
> Cover me, cover me, cover me.

I have already mentioned that the word *goel*, here translated near kinsman, is elsewhere translated redeemer (indeed, the noun and its verb are so translated 62 times in the Old Testament), and it is this title which Jehovah claims for Himself with regard to His people Israel. This is particularly so in the prophecy of Isaiah. Again and again Jehovah relates Himself to Israel as 'Thy Redeemer, the Holy One of Israel.' The interesting thing, however, is that this word does not occur at all in Isaiah until after chapter 40; but after that chapter it occurs in great profusion. The reason seems to be that up to chapter 40 the general theme is that of the judgement and captivity which the people's sin and their unwillingness to return to the Lord would make inevitable. From

[1] Titus 2:14 RV

chapter 40 onwards the judgement is not seen as future, but as having already fallen and the people are seen as already in captivity. Immediately God 'changes His tune,' if I may put it that way, and speaks only of the grace that comes to them in their need, and the glorious restoration of themselves and their land that He has for them. It is as if He says, 'It is enough; I will not contend for ever, neither will I be always wroth.' Then He begins to reveal Himself as their *goel*, their Redeemer, and to tell them that though the worst has come to the worst, He will yet redeem. It is as if He is saying, 'Everything has gone wrong for you and that for your own sin; but what of that? Is My hand shortened at all that it cannot now redeem, or have I no power to deliver?' I think I can hear those who receive this message answering in surprise, 'We always knew You could redeem, but we never thought You would; for it has all been so much our own fault.' And in reply Jehovah seems to say, 'I am thy *Goel*, thy Redeemer, made for such a situation as this.'

I mention this point because it is only when things have gone wrong, even when the worst has come to the worst, that Jesus comes into His own as our nearest Kinsman with the right to redeem. Indeed, when Jesus comes to a life, He does not expect to find things right; and usually He is not disappointed in His non-expectations. If nothing has gone wrong, then there is nothing for Him to redeem. He is made for just the situation in which you, dear one, may find yourself. And the very word, redeemer, should help here. It not only begins with the prefix 're' it also ends with the suffix 'er'. There are, of course, many words that end this way—work*er*, driv*er*, writ*er*. A work*er* is a man who does not work just once, but who continually works; a driv*er* is one who habitually drives; and a writ*er* is one who continually writes. And so of the word Redeem*er*; He is not One Who redeems just once, and that's it; He is One Who habitually and continually redeems. Whenever things go wrong, He is there as our Redeemer, and if things go wrong again on the same

point or in another matter, He is ready to make it good again.
As we have seen, 'again' is implied in the prefix 're'; both
prefix and suffix speak of a continual redemption. What an
encouragement, then, for us to be quick to repent and avail
ourselves of Him!

All this means that we need be no longer afraid of sin. It is,
of course, always a healthy thing to be afraid *to* sin (remember Joseph's answer to Potiphar's wife[1]), but we are speaking here of not being afraid *of* sin. Some people are so fearful
lest they fail that they are all the time holding on tight and,
of course, that very attitude predisposes them to fail. They
are like a rabbit which, terrified and fascinated by a snake,
because of its very terror, walks right into the snake's jaws
(do snakes have jaws?). We need not be like that. We know
what to do with sin; we know One Who has the answer, Who,
if things do go wrong, knows how to redeem and set us free
from guilt and the tyranny of self-recrimination.

> Dear dying Lamb, Thy precious blood,
> Shall never lose its power.

Such confidence in the power of the blood of Jesus, far
from giving us licence to sin, gives us courage and strength
to say 'No'. But if a person feels that everything depends on
him walking the knife-edge of victory and that if he falls off
everything is finished, then indeed he is finished! But things
are never finished for the one who knows the power of his
nearest Kinsman to redeem again.

To conclude this chapter, we remind ourselves that the
Hebrew of old did not have to wait until the year of jubilee to
have his lands restored and himself set free from slavery. If
he had a near kinsman who was able and willing he could
have both his lands and himself redeemed right away. There
is, indeed, a jubilee celebration waiting for us in heaven,
when every last thing will be made good and every tear be

[1] Gen. 39:9

dried. But we do not have to wait till then to have the losses of sin made good, our tears dried, our problems solved. Inasmuch as Jesus is our nearest Kinsman, we can enjoy a full redemption long before that jubilee. We don't have to go on with our sighs, we don't have to continue with those inner failures and traits that daunt us, we don't have to settle for anything less than what is promised in the Word of God. There are unexplored areas in the redemption of our Lord Jesus that we have yet to discover.

Note: This word *goel*, translated in some places 'near kinsman', in yet more places 'redeemer', is yet in other places translated 'avenger', as in the phrase, 'the avenger of blood' (Joshua 20:3, etc). This shows another side of the work of a *goel*; it was not only to redeem on behalf of his brother, but in the event of him being murdered, to avenge his brother by slaying the murderer. 'Whoso sheddeth man's blood, by man shall his blood be shed' was the command of Genesis 9:6, and the one to carry out that sentence was the *goel*. When therefore Jehovah is said to be the Redeemer of Israel, it means also that He is the Avenger of Israel. Indeed, in the Old Testament, He redeems Israel by taking vengeance on those who are oppressing her. His mercy to Israel is shown by His judgement of her foes. This explains a passage like Isaiah 63:1–7, which begins with a tremendous show of strength on God's part against His and Israel's enemies, and which uses such expressions as 'tread them in mine anger,' and 'trample them in my fury,' and 'their blood sprinkled upon my garments.' This is immediately followed by the dulcet tones of Israel's praises, 'I will mention the lovingkindnesses of the Lord, and the praises of the Lord, according to all that the Lord hath bestowed upon us.' Quite clearly, the Lord's mercy to Israel here is shown by His judgement on her oppressors. Indeed, the two concepts are brought together in verse 4, 'for the day of vengeance is in Mine heart and the year of My redeemed is come.' It can be said that the Lord Jesus redeems us in the same way, by taking vengeance on our foes, sin, death and Satan in His cross. We can almost put into His mouth the same words with regard to these foes that have oppressed us, 'The day of vengeance is in mine heart, and the year of my redeemed is come.'

CHAPTER 4

RUTH, A GLEANER IN THE FIELD OF BOAZ

'Go not to glean in another field . . .'

As we have turned the pages of this story, it has been first Naomi and then Boaz who has claimed our attention. Now we turn to Ruth, the one after whom the book is named. The story of the young poverty-stricken widow from Moab who became a princess in Israel and an ancestress of Jesus Christ, has almost the air of a fairy-story romance about it. And if you did not realise that she indeed became an ancestress of Jesus Christ, turn to Matthew chapter 1 where you find her name enshrined in the genealogy of the Messiah on His human side. But more of that later.

Everything for her began when she made the momentous decision in the fields of Moab to follow her mother-in-law back to Bethlehem-Judah. 'Intreat me not to leave thee, or to return from following after thee: for whither thou goest, I will go; and where thou lodgest, I will lodge: thy people shall be my people, and thy God my God: where thou diest, will I die, and there will I be buried.' The natural thing was for her to do what her sister-in-law, Orpah, did—go back to her own people and her ancient gods, where she would always feel at home and where she might find another husband. Indeed, Naomi expected her to return there and counselled her in her own interest to do so. And we could not blame her if she had, for after all she had no blood ties with Naomi, just the 'accident,' so to speak, of a few months marriage to her son. Moreover, Naomi herself confessed that she had nothing to offer her. But Ruth chose otherwise and a momentous choice it was. It meant going to Bethlehem with nothing, with no prospect but to share Naomi's poverty. It meant, above all, going to live amongst an utterly strange people, whose ways and customs she would not know. Indeed, it was not at all clear to what extent the proud Israelites would welcome a Gentile to live amongst them. And yet she chose it.

As we look closer at her words, we find her decision was really compounded of three distinct choices which were in a progressive order. It would appear at first sight that she began by deciding to follow Naomi back to her land and was prompted by love and loyalty to do so. She then went on to choose Naomi's people to be her people, for now she would have to live among them. And if that also meant that their God would have to be her God, then she would be willing for that too, and would try to conform. I want to suggest, however, that the order of Ruth's choices was actually the reverse of this, and that she did not begin by being attracted to Naomi so much as to Naomi's God, the One Naomi called Jehovah. As explained in a previous chapter, Ruth discovered Him to be the sinner's God, the God of grace, and therefore she chose Him. From there she went on to choose His people, saying, in effect, 'If there is a people whose God is Jehovah and who live under the beneficence of His grace, happy is the people that is in such a case; that people shall be my people and as I live among them, maybe something of what they experience I will find too.' Then, of course, she went on to cleave to Naomi herself, in whose tears of repentance she caught her first glimpse of the God of grace. And even when she got to Bethlehem and found the only way to get food enough to live was to be a menial gleaner, she was content. There was a lot of difference between a reaper and a gleaner. A reaper was a recognised worker, receiving wages; a gleaner had no such status; he or she was just one of the poor in the land, allowed to pick up the stray bits of grain left by the reapers. and this was the low place that Ruth took. Even so, as I say, she was content, and I like to think that she whispered blissfully to herself, as she went about her lowly task, 'Better to be a gleaner among such a people, with such a God, than a well-paid reaper anywhere else.'

I trust what I have written to amplify Ruth's thinking and

responses commends itself to the reader; for myself, the more I ponder it, the more sure I am it is all implied in the sacred text. In any case, there is something for the Christian here. Deeper things for him often begin in the same way. He comes across people in whom he finds incarnated the very blessing he needs and who seem to have a peace and radiance that he has not yet found in his Christian life. As he gets close to them and hears them sharing their experiences, he finds them often repenting, and taking the sinner's place at the foot of the cross, from whence they appear to derive all their joy and liberty. He had assumed that theirs was the good person's God, that they had had to attain certain high standards and to fulfil stringent conditions to be so blessed; as for him, he just cannot make it. But as he listens it dawns on him that such is not the case; theirs is the sinner's God, the God of grace and all that has happened to them is they have learned to live on the ground of grace in a way he has not. And he begins to get a new vision of Jesus, and to see He has something infinitely good for failed saints, if they will confess that is what they are. As a result he desires that their God, the sinner's God, should be his God, for he sees he qualifies, if only by his sins. And he goes further and says to himself, 'If there is a people who know the blessedness of living this way, then that people shall be my people; I want to sit among them and see what they see and maybe something of what they have will rub off on me.' And he begins to take his place amongst them, just as a gleaner in the field of grace, a seeker after the truth, not yet a finder. It is a very humbling thing for a man to do this and to confess that there is something missing in his Christian life, especially if that man is in any degree a leader; but this is the way to begin. The first step to have to fuller Christian life is to confess that you have not got it. Be very definite about this.

At the opening meeting of a conference of Christian workers we were each invited to introduce ourselves and to say why we had come. I shall never forget one **minister** saying,

'I am the unsuccessful vicar of an unsuccessful parish.' He
had the humility to declare that he had come just as a seeker,
not yet a finder. Was there a better candidate for grace than
that man? I once met an American missionary in a distant
land who had gone there with a very specialised ministry
along a certain line of truth. The Lord worked deeply in all
our meetings, and he saw and heard many repenting of sin
before the Lord and sharing with one another the consequent experience of grace into which they were entering. He
saw the sinner's God in action, and in the light of it he
realised that what he had before was largely only theory. He
said to me, 'This is what I want. You tell me there is a
conference away in England where you folks learn together
these things and are living this way; may I come and sit with
you all?' He was willing to come thousands of miles just to be
a gleaner among those who had seen that their God was the
God of grace and were walking with Him on that basis.

HEARTS TOUCHED

This momentous choice on Ruth's part impressed everyone
in Bethlehem and she became known as 'the Moabitish
damsel that came back with Naomi out of the country of
Moab.' It touched them, not only because she had returned
with Naomi, but also because she had given up so much just
to be one of them and to take refuge under the wings of their
God; and they were drawn to her. News of what the Gentile
girl had done reached Boaz too and it apparently made a
profound impression on him, even before she appeared in
his fields. How impressed he was can be gathered from his
words to her at that first meeting: 'It hath fully been showed
me, all that thou hast done unto thy mother-in-law since the
death of thine husband; and how thou hast left thy father and
thy mother, and the land of thy nativity, and art come unto a
people which thou knewest not heretofore. The Lord
recompense thy work, and a full reward be given thee of the
Lord God of Israel, under Whose wings thou art come to

trust.' Quite clearly what drew him to her in the first place was not that she was possibly young and attractive, or even that he was a near kinsman to the family with the right to redeem (that fact had not yet dawned on either of them), but simply the touching choice she had made with its moral and spiritual overtones.

As a result when, to quote, 'her hap was to light on a part of the field belonging unto Boaz,' he took special note of her and extended to her unusual favours not normally accorded to gleaners. First, he welcomed her into his fields and told her to glean in no other. Usually farmers only tolerated gleaners, not welcomed them. Next he gave her permission to drink of the vessels provided for the reapers; gleaners normally had no such right. Further, he assured her that he had charged his young men not to make improper advances to her, or molest her. Then at noon he invited her to eat with him and his reapers, to take of the bread and dip it in the vinegar. Farmers never regarded themselves under any obligation to provide food for the gleaners; they just remained hungry till the end of the day. But Boaz did more than invite her to eat with them; he personally 'reached her parched corn,' and that in such quantity that she was not only satisfied herself, but also had something over to take back to her mother-in-law. Finally, he instructed his reapers to let her glean right amongst the sheaves. Usually, if gleaners got as close as that they were told gruffly to clear off. But Boaz told them to let her do it 'and reproach her not.' He goes even further and whispers to the reapers 'and let fall also some of the handfuls of purpose for her, and leave them, that she may glean them.' And for the second time he adds the words, 'and rebuke her not.' What a man, Mr. Great-Heart, if ever there was one!

The result was that Ruth found the fields of Boaz to be fields of grace indeed. Gleaners worked long to gather little; but she was gathering much with little effort. Ruth was overwhelmed with the grace of it and she, quite literally, 'fell on her face and bowed herself to the ground,' and asked him why, why, why; 'Why have I found grace in thine eyes, seeing I am a stranger?' For answer he only said, 'It hath been fully showed me, all that thou hast done.' If someone said that to us, we would feel a bit uneasy and expect him to go on to enumerate our secret sins; not so Boaz, he went on to enumerate those deep and costly choices which she had made in all her poverty and which had touched him so much. And choking a little, I think, he added, 'The Lord recompense thy work, and a full reward be given thee of the Lord God of Israel under whose wings thou art come to trust.'

The magnanimity of Boaz to the poor gleaner, Ruth, is nothing to be compared to the vast grace of the Lord Jesus toward the one who is humble enough to confess himself a failed Christian and takes the sinner's God to be his God. Once we start taking that ground, we find ourselves the object of His special attention in a way that is not the case when we are protesting our sufficiency. As we bow before Him in our acknowledged failure and poverty, knowing that only Jesus can do the sinner any good, we find love, encouragement and help coming to us from every direction in a way that is quite extraordinary and quite undeserved. Handfuls of precious promises are left on purpose all over the place, and as we stoop to gather them we hear the words sounding again and again, 'Reproach her not, reproach her not.' And we find that, though we are but poor gleaners, the field in which we are gleaning is indeed the field of grace; for Jesus is doing things for us that we neither expected nor deserved, and they are but the presage of more to come. This really is the truth and not poetic fancy. The New Testament says, 'God sent not His Son into the world to condemn the world, but that the world through Him might be saved,' and if He is not condemning the world, He is certainly not condemning the failed saint who is honest enough to take his place as such. The records of God's dealings in the Old and New Testaments with sinners who have turned to Him, from Manasseh the wickedest of kings, to the woman taken in adultery, all proclaim the fact that God delights in mercy.

If confused and overwhelmed by such grace we ask, as Ruth did, 'Why have I found grace in Thine eyes that thou shouldest take notice of me, seeing I am what I am?' He will reply much as Boaz did to Ruth, 'It hath been fully showed me all that thou hast done. . . .' and He will point back, not so much to our sins as showing what we have done, but rather to our sighs over our sins, to the beginnings of a new honesty about ourselves and to the feeble faith that dares to hope that surely 'there is plentiful redemption in the blood that hath been shed.' This is what attracts Him to our aid. Sometimes He comes to us and says:

'I've come in answer to your prayer!'

'But I haven't prayed, Lord,' we reply, 'I've been too weak to pray.'

'Did you sigh?' He asks.

'Yes, Lord, I certainly sighed.'

'Then that was your prayer,' He says, 'and I have come in answer to it.'

NATHANAEL UNDER THE FIG TREE

It was much the same in the case of Nathanael. Jesus spoke of him as if He knew all about him saying, 'Behold, an Israelite indeed, in whom is no guile;' and yet Nathanael had never met Him before.

'Whence knowest thou me?' Nathanael asked, quite naturally.

'Before that Philip called thee, when thou wast under the fig tree, I saw thee,' Jesus replied.

That startled Nathanael, because that place under the fig tree was, I rather think, the most private place in the world to him. That was the place where he went when he wanted to be alone and think. But Jesus knew what had been going on under that fig tree, and apparently what happened there that day made it possible for Him to say, 'Behold, an Israelite indeed, in whom is no guile.'

Notice He did not say, 'in whom is no sin,' but 'in whom is no guile,' that is, no hiding of sin. Well, what do you think went on under that fig tree? I can only infer that there Nathanael had been facing the truth about himself, that he had been confessing as much as he knew about himself to as much as he knew of God. He might not have got much further than this at that time and been only a seeker rather than a finder, but it was this that attracted the grace of God to him and enabled Jesus to speak of him in the terms He did. What had gone on under that fig tree was known only to God and, therefore, Nathanael reasoned, the One Who now spoke to him and revealed His knowledge of him must be Deity, and he confessed, 'Thou art the Son of God, Thou art the King of Israel.'

To suggest that there can be something in us that attracts the grace of God may raise a question in our minds. Someone may say, 'But I thought that grace did not have to find anything in us to be attracted to us. I thought that grace was God's love for those in whom there is nothing good; otherwise grace is no longer grace.' But what is it we have suggested attracts grace, if it is not simply the confession there is nothing good in us, nothing to attract. That is the one thing that can be in us without grace ceasing to be grace. Indeed, where there is this acknowledgment, we make ourselves quite ostensibly candidates for grace in a way that we could not be as long as we thought everything was fine with us. If grace is the love of God for the guilty, it implies that we have to admit we are guilty in order to qualify for what is offered. If it is true that 'God justifies the ungodly,' it implies we recognise we are ungodly in order for Him to justify us. And the moment we cease to fight against the truth and agree with God, we become fit candidates for that

> Marvellous grace of our loving Lord,
>   Grace that exceeds our sin and our guilt,
> Yonder on Calvary's mount outpoured,
>   There where the blood of the Lamb was spilt.

So it was the very fact that Ruth was a Gentile and a foreigner, and yet had chosen Jehovah to be her God and His people to be her people, that drew Boaz to her. And he knew all that about her before she ever knew him. As we think of God's foreknowledge of us under our fig trees, we must surely say with David, 'Such knowledge is too wonderful for me; it is high, I cannot attain to it.'[1]

'GLEAN NOT IN ANOTHER FIELD'

In view of the fact that Ruth had begun to find such grace at the hands of Boaz, we are in a position to understand the importance of his words to her: 'Go not to glean in another field, neither go from hence, but abide here fast by my maidens.' How inappropriate it would have been, if having received so much kindness and abundance in his field, she was to try some other field in the hope she would find more there. Even Naomi, when told of all that had happened, gave her the same counsel, 'It is good, my daughter, that thou go out with his maidens, that they meet thee not in any other field.' What she meant was, how embarrassing it would be for you if, having received such good treatment in their field, they should find you in another field. What reproachful looks they would give you, and what aspersions it would seem to cast on the man, as if what he had done was not enough, or might not continue. The fact was that the field of Boaz held infinitely more promise for her than any other field in Israel, as the event showed.

This is an important word for us too; go not to glean in any other field than the field of grace; seek not any other answer save that which is found at the foot of the cross of Jesus. Of course, to continue to glean in the field of grace involves you in continuing to repent, if not over one thing, then over another. The cross is not for anything else than sin, and to continue in the field of grace you must often have recourse to it. You may, however, feel restive in this path of constant

[1] Psalm 139:6

acknowledgment of need, and tell yourself that in continuing this way you are not getting anywhere; where is victory? But continue there, dear one, glean not in any other field, seek not to add anything to Jesus and His finished work on the cross for your peace. Ultimately He will meet you there and give you an experience of redemption and revival, and that in a continuing way—more than you ever hoped for. Ruth never dreamed that the one in whose field she was gleaning was a near kinsman, a *goel*, one destined to redeem the family losses and bring them into great wealth; but thus it happened. So as the old hymn says, 'Cling to the cross, the burden will fall.' Things may not happen immediately as you desire, but be assured, if they do not happen there they will not happen anywhere else. But the burden will fall and everything else come right, if you stay there and glean not anywhere else.

Yes, there are other fields in which we can glean, if we are determined to do so, alternative ways to that of grace. It would not be right to suggest here what these other fields might be. In any case, what constitutes 'another field' will vary from person to person and from situation to situation. Only the Holy Spirit can show you when you are trying to glean in another field than the field of grace. Although the alternatives to the way of grace may differ greatly from one another, they have nearly all one thing in common. They invariably speak to us as something other than sinners and propose things for us to do which are beyond us as such. There are rules to keep, experiences to gain, steps to take, if we are to become victorious; but it seems to be forgotten we are too weak to take the first step, let alone the rest. The result is that we are put under strain, and are struggling in our own strength and never make the grade. This, in turn, implies that Jesus is not enough for the sinner and we are in effect adding something to Him—if not something for us to do, then some feeling for us to experience. And invariably what is added to Him becomes more important than He Himself, and makes Him of none effect to us. All these additions to Christ are really only subtle variants of the way of works, about which Paul has so much to say in his epistles. How embarrassing for those of us who have 'begun in the Spirit' to be found by our brothers in another field, seeking to be 'made perfect by the flesh'![1] But we have all done it in one degree or another and have sometimes gained for ourselves the reputation of those who are always off on some new thing. The new thing only leads to despair and frustration. What rest to return to the field of grace and to the foot of the cross, where everything is made available as a gift to the poor man who confesses himself to be poor.

And so it was Ruth resigned herself to go to no other field than the one where she had begun. However, at this point in the story, she is still only a gleaner; the larger destiny that is in store for her had not been thought of, much less experienced. But she has at least learnt the name of the one in whose field she has been gleaning. When asked by Naomi in the evening, 'Where hast thou gleaned today?' she replied, 'The man's name with whom I wrought today is Boaz.' That was the first time that name had ever been on her lips. She little knew how dear it was to become to her, nor how much the bearer of it was to do for her. In coming days she was going to have good cause to sing,

> How sweet the name of Boaz sounds,
>   In a poor gleaner's ear!
> It soothes her sorrows, heals her wounds,
>   And drives away her fear.

[1] Gal. 3:3

CHAPTER 5

RUTH AT THE FEET OF BOAZ

'And, behold, a woman lay at his feet . . .'

When Ruth told her mother-in-law that the name of the man in whose field she had been gleaning was Boaz, I like to think that Naomi suddenly sat bolt upright. At the sound of that name she realised two things that could have tremendous bearing on their situation. She said, 'The man is near of kin unto us, one of our next kinsmen.' The two things she realised were bound up with the two phrases she used, 'near of kin unto us' and 'one of our next kinsmen'. The Authorised Version obscures for us the fact that there are two quite different Hebrew words here with quite different meanings; even the Revised Standard Version does not help us to see this distinction. In the first phrase the Hebrew word *qarob* is used which simply means a relative. Well, of course, that was something to cause Naomi to prick up her ears and make a comment. 'Boaz is one of my husband's relatives,' she said, 'how interesting that you should have found yourself gleaning in his fields of all fields!' It was for a moment just an interesting coincidence to Naomi. She had presumably known him as one of the large family, but she had never been close to him, and in the years of her former prosperity he had never meant anything to her. Since then she had lost touch with him, but he was a relative nonetheless. But it was the second word she used which showed that what she was hearing was not merely interesting, but vitally important to them. The phrase she used was 'one of our next kinsmen', and here 'kinsman' is in the Hebrew another word altogether, *goel*, the word we have already talked so much about. The Authorised Version does actually try to help us here, because in its margin we have, 'Or, *one that hath the right to redeem*.'

She saw that not only was he a relative, but because of that fact he had the right to redeem for them. More, she saw that their very loss of all and the childless widowhood of Ruth qualified them to invoke the law of the *goel*. Little wonder that Naomi got quite excited as she tried to explain the ancient Hebrew law to Ruth. Little wonder that she urged Ruth not to be found gleaning in any other field than that of Boaz, for already there was forming in her mind a plan as to how this right, vested in Boaz, might be invoked on their behalf. But this was not merely a legal matter, but a matter of the heart. There would have to grow up a mutual love between Boaz and Ruth. So everything had to be done carefully in just the right way at just the right time.

We, too, need a like revelation of the right vested in the Lord Jesus for us, if we are to be emboldened to put in our plea for the full redemption that grace has for us. We need to see that the One who has been showing us such undeserved favours ever since we took our place as gleaners in His field has more and is more. We need to see that Jesus is our nearest Kinsman, with the right to redeem both ourselves and our situation, a right acquired through the mighty sufficiency of His blood. The Son of man has the right on earth to forgive sins, and more, to redeem and overrule for ultimate good the very losses occasioned by our sin. And it is all based on blood, in the shedding of which all blame attaching to us was anticipated and extinguished.

With that vision of the blood must go a new vision of grace—that our very lacks, faults and failures are our qualifications for what grace provides, in the same way that Ruth had to see that her poverty and widowhood were the very things that qualified her for a redeemer. The lines of John Newton's hymn,

> Thou callest burdened souls to Thee,
> And such, O Lord, am I,

always give me afresh, as I sing them, this vision of grace.

They show me that Jesus specialises in burdened souls and calls such to Him, and that being the case, I qualify, 'for such, O Lord, am I.' Our situations of need are not our disqualification as the Devil would have us to believe, but are in fact, if duly acknowledged, our only qualification to be blessed, which means we are just the case for Him. A new vision of the blood of Christ and the grace of God, then, is all important if we want to make the same daring claim on our nearest Kinsman, as Ruth made on hers. So do yourself the luxury of hearing again and again this sweet Gospel; and if it does not seem to come always from the pulpit, then start preaching it to your heart yourself, until at last you have the boldness to lie at the feet of your Kinsman with great confidence as to what He will do for you.

'SPREAD THY SKIRT OVER ME!'

At last Naomi is ready with her plan. She can see something better for Ruth than merely being a gleaner, coming back each evening tired out with her work in the fields. She can see her in her own home, loved and honoured as wife and mother. This is what she meant when she said to her one evening, 'my daughter, shall I not seek rest for thee (RSV, a home for you) that it may be well with thee?' And when Ruth evinces surprise at such a prospect, she said, 'Is not Boaz of our kindred, with whose maidens thou wast?' And then she revealed her plan to send her to him to invoke the law of the *goel*. But it was a most delicate matter, for while Boaz had the right to redeem, he might not want to; it involved more than redeeming land; it involved taking on a woman. But Naomi had good reason to believe that Boaz was touched, perhaps much more than touched, by the lowly gleaner in his fields, and with a woman's intuition she knew that Ruth on her part had come to love this Mr. Great-Heart.

Thus it was that Naomi instructed Ruth as to what she was to do. It was the end of barley harvest and there would be much merry-making down at the threshing-floor. Ruth was told to wash and anoint herself and put on new clothes. It is quite possible that up till then she had been wearing a widow's rags, and everybody would know her as such. But in changing her clothes she was in effect declaring for those who might see her that she was available to be married again. But she was not to be seen by any but one man. She was therefore to stand in the shadows and wait till the feast and merry-making were over and the people had gone home. She was to wait to see where Boaz laid himself down, because he had to sleep by the winnowed barley lest it should be stolen. She watched him as he composed himself in the shadows and drew his garment over him. When he was asleep, she stole in and, according to instructions, lifted the clothes that covered his feet and lay down there. I can only infer that Naomi's instructions to uncover his feet were to ensure that he would wake up, but slowly and naturally. Cold feet are sure to wake anybody up! But not with a rude shock. The sleeper would wake up slowly, not knowing at first what it was that was waking him. And this is just what happened. At midnight he woke, 'and behold, a woman lay at his feet.'

'Who art thou?' he said, startled.

'I am Ruth thine handmaid' she said 'spread therefore thy skirt over thine handmaid, for thou art a near kinsman.'

Now what was meant by spreading the skirt over another? There is a further passage where the same expression is used, Ezekiel 16:8, from which it is clear that it was a symbolic act by which a man would claim the one of his choice to be his wife. The passage in question is a beautiful parable showing how Jehovah had espoused Israel to be His; 'Now when I passed by thee and looked upon thee, behold, thy time was the time of love, and I spread my skirt over thee ... and thou becamest mine.'

Now normally it was the place of the man to do the spreading of the skirt, for he had to make the choice. Not many a girl would feel she could ask the man to spread his skirt over her, because it would be tantamount to her proposing to him. But that is exactly what Ruth did here. In saying, 'Spread thy skirt over thine handmaid,' she was saying in effect, 'Marry me, marry me, Boaz. Take me on as your wife.' This was purely a symbolic act, understand; there is no hint in this story of any invitation to Boaz to act improperly towards her. But even so, if it meant Ruth was asking Boaz to marry her, it certainly seems immodest, to say the least, and quite out of place. But wait a moment, she gives the reason for her request, 'for thou art a near kinsman—a *goel*,' that is, one that had the right to redeem the lost estates of Mahlon and to take on his widow in order to raise up seed in his name. The moment she said, 'for thou art a *goel*,' that changed everything; there was nothing improper in what she had done; she was simply invoking the law of the *goel* on her behalf, and Boaz knew it. She was not to be blamed at all in making this advance; if anyone was to be blamed, it was Boaz in not realising he stood in this special relationship to her. And he responded immediately, 'It is true I am thy near kinsman. . . . I will do to thee all that thou requirest.'

Now that is what we have to do—go and lie at His feet. How moving it is, when it can be said of us, 'and behold a failed Christian lies at His feet'; or 'behold a failed preacher lies at His feet'; or 'behold a failed husband or wife lies at His feet'; or 'a failed father or mother'; or 'a failed young Christian who began so brightly lies at His feet.' And they have each gone there because they have seen that in spite of all, He is their nearest Kinsman, Who has the right, power and willingness to redeem all that has gone wrong, forgiving the sinner and taking over his situation. The simple truth is that you cannot be so wrong, or depressed, or your affairs so tangled and confused, but there is a place sanctified for you at His feet. And lying there you can pray Ruth's prayer, 'Spread Thy skirt over this sinner, take me on, bail me out, because Thou art my nearest Kinsman.'

When He sees you there and hears you talking like that, He knows He has got a sinner on His hands who is appealing to

His right and power to redeem—and He does not fail. Till you get to His feet and begin to repent, the situation you have either caused or contributed to is your responsibility. But once you lie at His feet with your sin and need, not only is the sin forgiven and its stain cleansed, but He also takes over the situation as His own responsibility.

Of course we are not always ready to see ourselves as failed Christians or to admit we have caused or contributed to the situation we are in. For myself, I find that even if I do not appear to be the one who has caused the problem, I have certainly contributed to it by my wrong reactions. If another person has done the wrong action in the first place, my reactions to him have been wrong too, and they have only made things worse. By the time an argument has been going on for some while it is difficult to know who was wrong in the first place, because both of us are so wrong now. Is it his unbrokenness or mine which is the trouble? As someone has said, 'When Christians quarrel, the Devil remains neutral and provides ammunition to both sides.'

Quite obviously, Jesus cannot 'spread His skirt over me' and take me and my situation on until I am prepared to lie at His feet as the wrong one, without waiting for anybody else to take that place first. Although we all hate to take our place as the wrong one, it is something we must learn to do, and it takes some learning. But practice makes perfect—or relatively so! But when we do take this place in a situation, He not only gives us peace and forgiveness, but proceeds to heal and make things new again—often even better than they were before.

Here we may well need the word that Naomi gave to Ruth, 'Sit still my daughter, until thou know how the matter will fall: for the man will not be in rest until he hath finished the thing.' There was a matter that Boaz had to deal with before he could proceed to do the part of a kinsman for Ruth (we shall look at that in the next chapter). We, too, having been to the foot of the cross, and laid our affairs out there, will sometimes have to sit still and wait while God works things out.

Whereas the forgiveness of sins and the restoration of the soul is immediate, His recovery operation with regard to our situation may proceed a little more slowly, because there are other factors that God needs to handle or other people upon whom He has to work. So, 'sit still, my daughter, for the Man will not be in rest until He hath finished the thing.' We can rest because He will not rest. But finish the matter He certainly will if we leave it with Him. This does not mean that He may not ask our obedience and cooperation in certain matters, it could be by way of confession or restitution or something else; but none of us should think that those acts in themselves are going to heal things. The redeeming of every-thing is another matter which only He can do, and is the sphere where He is gloriously expert. And so, 'Sit still, my daughter . . . the Man will not rest . . .'

THE RESPONSE OF BOAZ

Now what was the response of Boaz to this daring claim? Can you believe it—he thanked her! He said, 'Blessed be thou of the Lord, my daughter,' He was delighted that she had made her appeal to him as her *goel*, not because he loved her, though I believe he was in process of losing his heart to her, but because in all her poverty and foreignness she had had the boldness to appeal to this law of Jehovah, the God of grace. He said in effect, 'Thank you, thank you, for giving me the privilege of exercising my right as a near Kinsman Redeemer.'

And when you go to the foot of the cross for redemption and revival, Jesus thanks you for coming. This comes out in John 16:24, where Jesus says, 'Hitherto have ye asked nothing in My Name; ask, and ye shall receive, that your joy may be full.' Do you see it, He is asking us to ask! If he has one complaint against us more than another, it is that we haven't asked. Usually we think that prayer is somehow to be an attempt to conquer His reluctance, and the way we pray betrays that is how we feel about it. It is nothing of the sort;

it is rather a laying hold of His willingness. He is asking you
to ask, He is asking you to come and take Ruth's place, He is
asking you to present the mess to Him; and when you do, He
thanks you for the privilege. We thank Him, of course, but
nothing makes Him so happy as to see another one lying at
His feet and saying,

> Cover me, cover me,
>   Extend the border of Thy mantle over me,
> Because Thou art my nearest Kinsman,
>   Cover me, cover me, cover me.

And cover us with the mantle of His precious blood He
certainly does.

Now let us look in greater detail at all that Boaz said to
Ruth that day, because it is important. 'Blessed be thou of
the Lord, my daughter; for thou hast showed more kindness
in the latter end than at the beginning, inasmuch as thou
followedst not young men, whether poor or rich.' In referring
to the kindness which she had shown at the beginning, Boaz
quite obviously had in mind the big choice she had made to
leave her own country and family in order to cleave to Naomi.
That was a kindness indeed. But he says, 'Thou hast showed
more kindness in the latter end than at the beginning.' Now
what was the kindness she had shown at the latter end? For
answer, consider what many another young widow would
have done in her situation. Such an one would have said,
'There is no future for me here, just gleaning in other
people's fields, living in this ruined farmhouse, looking after
an ageing mother-in-law; I'll cut my losses and look for a
husband amongst one of the young men.' Now Ruth would
have had a perfect right to do this, but had she done it and
found another husband outside the family, Naomi would
have been deserted, the family lands would probably never
have been redeemed, there would certainly be no seed raised
up in Mahlon's name to inherit them, and the family of
Elimelech would have become extinct in Israel. But she did

not do that; she rather chose to stick by Naomi and that old dying family; and when this new opportunity occurred, she got a vision for its revival. She made her appeal to Boaz for the redemption of the family's lands and offered herself to be the mother of its heirs, if Boaz would take her on and do the kinsman's part. As Boaz saw it, instead of trying to set up a new family, she was out for the revival of the old. This was the kindness she had shown at the latter end, and it was this that so delighted Boaz.

Now the spiritual application is this. It is very natural to us, when things go wrong and our situation does not work out as we would like, to decide to cut our losses, close the chapter and start on another situation. But why have things not worked out in the old situation? Have we been entirely innocent there? And if not, then we only carry our problems into the new. If you are a problem, everything is a problem whether in the old or new. I believe that what delights the Lord Jesus is not for us to be wanting a new situation, but getting a vision for the revival of the old, and asserting, there is nothing too hard for Jesus, there is nothing that He cannot do right there. And if it is the revival of the old we are after, we may find that we have to be repenting at the cross as much as the other people.

This would have application to someone in a difficult church, either as a member or even as the minister. Because things are not happy or suitable there, the natural thing is to want to close that chapter and go to another church. I am not saying that it is always wrong to leave a church; sometimes God guides a person to do just that. But surely the better thing, that which would glorify God more, is for the church to be changed and revived, rather than for us to go to a new one. And if that were our vision we might have to see that we need to be revived as much as any other.

This may well have application to a marriage which has not been working out happily. Very often when things go wrong, a person goes to the divorce court instead of the cross.

People prefer to end things rather than see their own wrong and let Jesus mend things. God surely wants you, instead of finishing with the old and hoping for something new, to get His vision for the changing and renewing of the old. That, too, may mean that the change has to begin with you, rather than with the other. As has been said, it takes two to make a quarrel but one can make it up. Why should not that one be you? And when the Lord sees you moving in that direction, He is delighted and says, 'Blessed be thou of the Lord, my daughter! Thank you for the opportunity of allowing me to come in to mend things.'

This principle is capable of a host of applications, not only to these two situations, but to much, much else, from the smallest to the largest matters. It is always true that 'mending things is a lot more rewarding than ending things,' as is expressed in this song I once heard a Cockney character sing in a Christian musical:

> Are there any old homes to mend?
> Any old hearts to mend?
>   Any father or daughter
>   Don't get on as they oughter?
> Any old hurts and hates to mend?
>
> In a world of smash and grab
> Where we're handy at giving each other the jab,
>   Somebody needs to start
>   And learn the difficult art
> Of mendin' things, mendin' things,
> A lot more rewarding than endin' things:
>   For a world at war,
>   Or a mother-in-law,
> We need Someone for mendin' things.
>
> Once on a lonely hill,
> They got hold of a Feller they wanted to kill,
>   They decided to chuck Him out,
>   'Cos He would keep going about,
> Just mendin' things, mendin' things,

A lot more rewarding than endin' things,
   But He's still around
   Some people have found
Just going on mendin' things.*

  * By Rev. Alan Thornhill. Used by permission.

CHAPTER 6

BOAZ AND THE NEARER KINSMAN

'Howbeit there is a kinsman nearer than I.'

When Boaz told Ruth he was ready to do what she required, he had to add there was one obstacle to him acting immediately. 'And now it is true that I am thy near kinsman: howbeit there is a kinsman nearer than I.' This man had a prior right to redeem and he had to be given the first chance. 'If he will perform unto thee the part of a kinsman, well; let him do the kinsman's part: but if he will not do the part of a kinsman to thee, then will I do the part of a kinsman to thee, as the Lord liveth.'

Now we are seeing in this book of Ruth pictures of the Lord Jesus and the Gospel of which He is the centre. If Boaz is to be seen as a foreshadowing of the Lord as Redeemer, what are we to make of this nearer kinsman, who had a prior right? Here we cannot be dogmatic, but I think we can take it to be a picture of the law of God, which has a prior right on the sinner. And the right which the law of God has over the sinner is to condemn him.

Now this is not purely fantasy. I find to my great interest other writers on this passage view it this way. In any case, this much is clear, that although Boaz was more than willing to play the part of a redeemer to Ruth, he felt he could not do so illegally. The law stated that the *goel* was to be the *next* of kin and this man was nearer than Boaz, and the law had to be satisfied before Boaz could play the part of a redeemer to her.

As we have said, the law of God has a prior claim on the sinner, and the claim that it has is to condemn him. For consider, the law of God sets before us certain high standards, and calls us to obey its moral demands. They are expressed not only in the Ten Commandments given at Sinai, but also in the Lord's Sermon on the Mount and in the many moral injunctions in other parts of the New Testament. And the law points to these high standards and says, 'This do and thou shalt live.'[1] This means that if we keep its commands and attain its standards we shall have eternal life and all else we need in our spiritual lives. But that word also implies, 'This fail to do and thou shalt die.' And in the event every last one of us has failed to do what the law has commanded, and all it can do now is to condemn us. This means that the commandment which was ordained to life, had we kept it, we find to be unto death because we have failed to do so.[2]

To condemn, then, is all the law can do. This does not mean that those standards are abrogated for the Christian. They are to be fulfilled, but under grace in a different way. Under the New Covenant of grace God makes Himself responsible to put into us what He wants out of us—not of course without our co-operation. But under law the onus is on us, and if we fail to achieve the required standards we are condemned. This means that the law of God and its high standards, beautiful as they may be, cannot redeem those who have fallen down on them. In chapter 4 this nearer kinsman twice says, 'I cannot redeem it.' Perhaps he felt that to do so would have meant selling part of his own inheritance and thus impoverishing his heirs. But whatever the reason for his inability, the words 'I cannot redeem it' are deeply significant when we see him as a picture of the law, able to condemn but never to redeem. Indeed, I Corinthians 15:56 tells us that the law actually strengthens sin rather than weakens it. It says there that 'the strength of sin is the law,' meaning that the law gives sin added power to condemn us when we fail. We might have thought that it should have told us the strength of sin is temptation but the strength of holiness is the law. Nothing of the sort: the higher our standards the greater our sense of guilt and accusation when

[1] Rom. 10:5   [2] Rom. 7:10

we fail. All our promises to be better and our espousal of higher goals only give the Devil more opportunity to accuse us and put an even bigger stick in his hand with which to thrash us.

So it is, if Jesus is our Kinsman Redeemer, the law is our kinsman condemner, and Jesus cannot play the part of a Redeemer to us until He has first settled things with the law. You will remember that when the First Epistle of John tells us that if we confess our sins God forgives and cleanses them, it is careful to make the point that He is 'faithful and just' to do so.[1] He is not going to forgive us in such a way as to bring divine justice into disrepute. If God is going to 'justify the ungodly,'[2] a way must be found in which He can be, to use Paul's phrase in Romans 3, 'just and the justifier of him which believeth in Jesus.'[3] If Jesus is going to be the sinner's Friend, and blot out the sinner's guilt and undertake the sinner's mess, He must first satisfy the law of God. To settle things with the nearer kinsman took Boaz to the gate of the city where all such matters were dealt with. But what Jesus had to do to settle things with the law took Him outside the city to the place of disgrace, to die on a cross between two thieves, as if He was one Himself. The supreme thing he did there was to rob sin of its power to condemn us, and He did it by bearing the curse attached to the broken law Himself, thus exhausting it. Actually, the first Person Whom sin lost its power to condemn was Jesus. In Romans 6:10 there is a sentence which tells us just this: 'In that He died He died unto sin once.' It does not say there that He died *for* sin merely, but *to* sin; that is, He died to sin's power to condemn Him any longer for the multitude of sins He took upon Him. The moment His blood was shed, the moment He said 'It is finished,' Satan and the law could not hold Him any longer, because the price had been paid. Therefore, 'Up from the grave He arose'; there was no reason for Him to stay there any longer. But if the law has lost its power to condemn our

---

[1] I John 1:9   [2] Rom. 4:5   [3] Rom. 3:26

Substitute, it has likewise lost its power to condemn all those whose Substitute He was.

Now that the nearer kinsman has relinquished his claim on us, Jesus can in real deed take the place of our nearest Kinsman with an unchallengeable right to redeem. On our part, those of us with the most tender of consciences need have no qualms in receiving His redemption on the easy terms grace offers, for <u>He has fulfilled the law for us,</u>

> Thou hast fulfilled the law
> And we are justified,
> Ours the blessing, Thine the curse,
> We live for Thou hast died.

I want to extol the mighty power of the blood of Jesus. Its efficacy extends not only to the sin itself but to the hangover of shame. The situation a man has created for himself may still continue and be only in process of recovery, but the man in the middle of it can be at perfect peace with God. By the power of the blood of Jesus the element of guilt in the situation has been completely expunged, and he can pray with confidence and joy about it as if it had not been his fault at all, and expect God to work on his behalf. Though wars may still arise against him, he knows the blessedness of the man to whom the Lord imputeth not iniquity.[1] The consequence of what he has done has become for God just so much raw material, one might say neutral raw material, for Him to make a new thing of. By neutral, I mean there is nothing in the mess that man presents God with which now implies blame. There is just no black mark against him. All clay to a potter is shapeless to begin with, and our heavenly Potter is not going to find any more difficulty in making something of our shapelessness than His earthly counterpart does with his clay.

THE TESTIMONY OF DAVID

It was because of this that David could pray in Psalm 3 with such boldness and joy about the circumstances he was

[1] Rom. 4:6-8

in, when he was fleeing from Absalom. Nathan had told him that this very thing, trouble from among his own family, would be part of God's discipline because of his sin. And yet here in this psalm, which has the heading, 'A Psalm of David when he fled from Absalom,' he says, 'Thou art a shield for me; my glory, and the lifter up of mine head,' and again, 'I laid me down and slept; I awaked; for the Lord sustained me;' he goes on, 'I will not be afraid of ten thousands of people, that have set themselves against me round about,' and he concludes by anticipating in faith the deliverance God is going to give him; 'Thou hast smitten all mine enemies on the cheek bone; Thou hast broken the teeth of the ungodly.' How was it that he was able to be so confident in his God at such a time, and not rather go about like a dog with its tail between its legs? It was because he knew, ever since he heard Nathan say 'The Lord hath also put away thy sin,' that the element of his culpability had been completely taken away. He was therefore able without any self-recrimination to trust God to work something new and good for him in that situation. Which of course, God did. He was ultimately brought back to his throne, more loved and honoured than ever before and the days that followed became the best days of his life. It is indeed a story of vindication, but not of the man himself but rather of his faith in the grace of God; and the Lord was seen once again to be the sinner's God. As far as we are concerned, our understanding of the complete atonement of the blood of Jesus that blots out sin should give us even greater encouragement to have like faith in grace. Jesus really is our glory and the lifter up of our head, and because of confidence born of faith in the blood of Jesus, we can smile at all similar foes and adverse circumstances.

NO RIGHT TO CONDEMN

All this is pictured in an incident in this part of the story of Ruth where the matter of who was going to redeem Naomi's inheritance was under discussion in the gate. When the nearer kinsman decided to relinquish his right, he took off his shoe and gave it to Boaz. The actual verses read this way, 'Now this was the custom in former times in Israel concerning redeeming and exchanging; to confirm a transaction, the one drew off his sandal and gave it to the other, and this was the manner of attesting in Israel.' So when the next of kin said to Boaz, 'Buy it for yourself,' he drew off his sandal. Then Boaz said to the elders and to all the people, 'You are witnesses.'[1] To walk over a property in a shoe meant, presumably, that one had the right to possess it. But in taking off his shoe, the kinsman symbolically indicated that there and then he relinquished his right to buy that land and handed that right over to Boaz. As someone has said commenting on this verse, 'The law has no right to walk over (that is, to condemn) that which Christ has redeemed.' That's good, isn't it? But the law and Satan have been trying to, haven't they, and you have let them! But they have no right to. You can overcome the law that would condemn and Satan that would accuse by the blood of the Lamb, and to make the transaction really complete you can add the word of your testimony. The Devil does not like that; he likes it all locked up in our bosoms. But when we have so seen the power of the blood of Jesus to give us peace about a matter as to be able to share it as a testimony with another, then we know a new dimension of freedom. 'They overcame him (the Devil, the accuser of the brethren) by the blood of the Lamb and the word of their testimony.'[2]

> Abel's blood for vengeance
>   Pleaded to the skies,
> But the blood of Jesus
>   For our pardon cries.

> Oft as it is sprinkled
>   On our guilty hearts
> Satan in confusion
>   Terror struck departs.

[1] Ruth 4:7–9 RSV   [2] Rev. 12:11

Some time ago when I was in another country taking meetings, I was looking forward to seeing again a young minister whom I had known there years before and who had come to experience the way of living under grace and walking with Jesus. He happened to be one of the best interpreters in the country and I was anticipating with pleasure having him interpret for me again. However, he did not show up for a week or two, until finally he came to a ministers' conference. I greeted him warmly and said, 'You're going to translate for me, aren't you?' He was very diffident and not at all sure that he would. All the sparkle had gone out of him, and he had so lost the joy that had characterised him that I felt this was not the brother I had known. Well, he did translate for me, but it was evident he was not at ease. Then he shared with me what had happened. In the intervening years he had had domestic trouble, strains between him and his wife, and it was quite widely known amongst his minister friends. The Lord had helped and it had been resolved, but the shame of it was still there. And somehow he did not feel he could stand up on the platform beside me and interpret, when he knew they all knew. Shame had taken from him his boldness and he felt there was a black mark against him. As we shared together, he saw and appropriated the power of the blood of Jesus, not only to forgive the initial wrongs, but especially to cleanse the consequent shame, the sense of not being free with people ('what are they thinking?' etc.). He saw he now had a testimony to give, not so much about the original matter, but much more with regard to the bondage he had been in as a result, and from which Jesus had now freed him. In coming months he let it be known in one way or another that that was his testimony, and his brother ministers loved him. They began to feel, strangely, that he had something that they had not, and they invited him to preach for them here and there, and they encouraged him to take the lead in this and that area of his denomination. When my wife and I went again three years after this he arranged the whole tour for us and great blessing came to other churches and other ministers because of this new sight of the power of the blood of Jesus God had given him. There he was interpreting with joy by my side the very message that had set him free, and they all knew it had. What a *goel*, what a near Kinsman! He not only forgives the sin but transfigures the situation and gives us back more than we had lost.

LACKING ASSURANCE OF SALVATION?

As we close this chapter let us turn again to those words which Naomi addressed to Ruth when there was still anxious doubt about how this matter of the nearer kinsman would turn out, words to which we have already referred; 'Sit still, my daughter, until thou know how the matter will fall: for the man will not be in rest until he hath finished the thing this day.'

We have already seen the application of this as regards the necessity of sitting still and trusting Him, while He sees to the restoration of our affairs. As we have said, we can rest because He will not rest, and it is safe to leave it to Him. And so Ruth found.

There is, however, another important application of these words. Some have lacked for years assurance about their salvation. They have tried to come to Jesus, they have sought to let Him into their hearts, but they are still not sure how it is between them and God, they still hardly dare class themselves as saved, and this has often cost them anxious thought. It is basically a doubt as to their righteousness before God and as to what constitutes their righteousness. The natural thing in such a case is for them to think if they could do more, such as pray more, love more, serve more, give more, feel more, they would know themselves right with God; but the trouble is that they are not adequate to do these things. To such the message is almost the same as these words, but not quite—'Sit still, my daughter.' Yes, that is the same message; stop striving, stop trying to do more, hand it over to Him. But then the message is not 'the man will not rest till he has finished the thing,' but rather, the Man Christ Jesus *has* finished it. His work on the cross is a finished work, of sufficient value to put away all your sins and to set you completely right with God, and nothing you can do can add to that righteousness or make it more secure. As a result of having finished His work He has rested and He bids you to do the same. 'This Man, after He had offered one sacrifice for sins for ever, sat down on the right hand of God,'[1] and He wants you to sit down too. Gaze then upon the blood, see His work finished for you on the cross and accepted for you in heaven; believe it and know yourself saved! Look and live!

> Nothing either great or small,
>   Nothing, sinner, no.
> Jesus did it, did it all,
>   Long, long ago.
>
> When He from His lofty Throne
>   Stooped to do and die,
> Everything was fully done:
>   Listen to His cry.
>
> 'It is finished' yes, indeed,
>   Finished every jot:
> Sinner, this is all you need,
>   Tell me, is it not?
>
> Till to Jesus' work you cling
>   By a simple faith,
> Doing is a deadly thing,
>   Doing ends in death.
>
> Cast your deadly doing down,
>   Down at Jesus' feet:
> Stand in Him, in Him alone,
>   Gloriously complete.

[1] Heb. 10:12

CHAPTER 7

THE HAPPY ENDING

"Ruth the Moabitess have I purchased to be my wife . . ."

Now we come to the happy ending. All the world loves a story with a happy ending, and that is, perhaps, one of the reasons why the book of Ruth has always had a charm for those who have read it. No happy ending like this one—it outdoes that of almost every other story in the world.

And for us, too, the story of grace has a happy ending. There may be many testings and tears, many repentances and new comings to the cross ere Jesus completes the needed recovery operation in our affairs. But I want to tell you that the grace of God always has a happy ending—and the happy ending of God's story utterly outdoes that of any other for wonder, for joy, and for the fulfilment of those involved. Psalm 30:5 says that His anger, or if you prefer the word, His discipline—that which Naomi had been subject to—is only for a moment, but His favour for a lifetime.[1] When His hand is heavy upon you, it seems as if it will never end. But be assured, it is really only for a moment, as you will see when you look back. That which is going to last forever is His favour. 'Weeping may endure for a night,' as it did for Naomi, 'but joy cometh in the morning.' In the night of weeping you may be tempted to doubt and say, 'My way is hid from the Lord and my right is disregarded by my God.'[2] But you must take yourself to task and say, 'Why art thou cast down, O my soul? And why art thou disquieted within me? Hope in God: for I shall yet praise Him, Who is the health of my countenance, and my God.'[3] Without any doubt you are going to arrive at the 'happy issue out of all your afflictions,' which grace has planned for you. And it

[1] Ps. 30:5 RV (margin)   [2] Isa. 40:27 RSV   [3] Ps. 43:5

does plan such for you, otherwise grace would not be grace.

It was so with Job; what a time of many testings he had; he seemed to lose everything, first his possessions, then his children and then finally his health! But how happy was the ending! When he had gone through it all, when he had humbled himself and deeply repented,[1] 'the Lord blessed the latter end of Job more than his beginning.'[2] His health was fully recovered and his possessions were restored to him twice as much as before—yes, the inventory of his flocks and herds detailed in both the first and last chapters shows he ended up with precisely twice as many sheep, camels, oxen and she-asses as at the beginning. He was a wealthy man by any standards at the beginning; it is anybody's guess how much he was worth at the end! More than that, ten further children were born to him to replace the ten he had lost, and a special note is made of the fact that his three daughters were 'the best-lookin' gals in town'.[3] And his last 140 years were the best years of his life! God's chastening anger endured only for a moment, His favour for 140 years! A happy ending indeed!

Let me tell you, loud and clear, you may expect a bright tomorrow! If you believe that, events will prove your faith in grace to have been amply justified. Our God is the God of the happy ending; He will do better unto you than at your beginnings.[4] Grace prophesies nothing but good ultimately for the man who knows how to lie at the feet of his nearest Kinsman as the one who has been wrong. He cannot speak such good of the unbroken one, who will not take that place. But let a man have but a measure of the broken and contrite heart, and God only speaks of the infinite good He intends to do for such a one. Encourage your heart, then, dear tested one; with Jesus there is a happy ending—yes, in this life, and much more so in the year of jubilee, when we stand with Christ in glory with everything culminated and every loss made good.

[1] Job 42:6   [2] Job 42:12   [3] Job 42:15   [4] Ezek. 36:11

So we see in this last chapter the ultimate union of the brideless Boaz and the widowed Ruth, two lonely people joined in a beautiful marriage. Ruth was lonely quite obviously; but I believe Boaz was lonely too. He was not a young man and yet had not found a bride. True he had to pay money to obtain Ruth, as he himself said, 'Ruth the Moabitess, the wife of Mahlon, have I purchased to be my wife.' But what was that compared to the joy of finding someone to share his life with. And in addition to this, the family lands of Mahlon were saved to be inherited by any seed they might have.

All this is but a faint reflection of the biggest union of all, that of the lonely sinner and, dare we say it, the lonely Saviour. Certainly, apart from those who make up the church Jesus Christ is brideless. It must be so, for with a big price He was willing to purchase you; do you remember the text, 'the church of God which He hath purchased with His own blood'?[1] And you are part of that church, that bride. And when you come to His cross there is a beautiful experience of the lonely unhappy sinner being joined to the Saviour Who is ever looking for the bride. Of course, when we were first saved we knew this, but we haven't been much in the way of spouses since then, have we? But the whole thing can be renewed again at His cross, and when necessary, again after that.

Now I want you to consider what the people said on this occasion. Their enthusiasm was immense; theirs was not a grudging acceptance of Ruth; they had watched the whole story as it had unfolded; they had admired the humility of this Gentile girl and they were so happy for Boaz that he had found a bride at last. Once the transaction with the nearer kinsman was completed and he had given his shoe to Boaz, the people began to express with great joy their felicitations to Boaz and Ruth. Notice some of the things they said.

[1] Acts 20:28

'WE ARE WITNESSES!'

When Boaz said to them, 'Ye are witnesses that I have bought Ruth to be my wife,' they all cried, 'We are witnesses.' Actually, in the Hebrew the words 'we are' do not appear; they just shouted the one word—'Witnesses!' They declared themselves witnesses of a beautiful act of the grace of God. This leads me to a text in the Acts of the Apostles which says, 'To Him give all the prophets witness, that through His Name whosoever believeth in Him shall receive remission of sins.'[1] And not only did the prophets bear witness to this great redemption but the Father from heaven bore witness too and on more than one occasion spoke audibly,[2] 'This is My Son, this is the Redeemer I have sent into the world.' And not only the Father, but a great company of others, for when we see this sort of thing happen in a life we too shout, 'witnesses!' There is nothing that rejoices our hearts so much as to see grace triumph in another life.

NO MORE A STRANGER

And then notice that they say, 'the Lord make the woman that is come into thine house . . .' What a beautiful way to describe this Gentile—no mention here of her earlier background of being a Moabitess. All that was of Moab about her had died, so to speak, when she was united to Boaz. She is never afterwards in the remaining verses called a Moabitess. And so with us. When we are first joined to Christ, or when we come again to Him, no mention is made of our sad past. The old man, that is the man of old, is regarded as finished with Christ on the cross long ago.

Ruth has no longer any cause to say what she said at first to Boaz in the fields, 'Why dost thou take notice of me, seeing I am a stranger, I am not like thine other handmaids.' She is no longer a stranger, she is really adopted into the common-

---

[1] Acts 10:43   [2] Matth. 3:17; 17:5. John 12:28

wealth of Israel. And so with you too. Till you get right with the Lord you feel you are different, not like the other Christians, you don't really belong. But once you take a sinner's place and you share your new experience of Jesus, you are no more a stranger; you are one of those who are but sinners around the Saviour.

This is the way into fellowship with other Christians. Sometimes people feel 'outside.' In East Africa one of the great criticisms by those who have not been in sympathy with the revival is that the revival fellowship has been exclusive. There were some missionaries who never felt that they were quite accepted, but others were. The reason was simple— some would not come into the sinner's fellowship by the only way there is, that of taking a sinner's place themselves and sharing a sinner's testimony. When a person does this, he finds himself brought into whatever sweet and caring fellowship there is; he cannot be more 'in' than the blood of Jesus brings him.

On my first visit to East Africa to link up with the revival brethren, I was asked to give a message at a big revival convention. I was surprised because I thought I was there only to learn. At three points in my message, I illustrated what I was trying to say by personal testimony, showing three instances in which I had been shown as a sinner who needed to come to the cross. At each of these three points in my message the meeting broke out into song and I just had to wait till they finished singing, 'Tuketendereza Yesu' (We praise you, Jesus). I did not hear them singing 'Tukutendereza' when I was expounding Scripture, though it was doubtless appreciated, but once I took a sinner's place, it was as if they were saying, 'Hallelujah, he's one of us!' Yes, that is the way in. And then, like Ruth, we are no more strangers, we really belong.

LIKE RACHEL AND LEAH

Then notice what else they said. 'The Lord make the

woman who is come into thy house like Rachel and like Leah!' These two wives of Jacob were the foundation mothers of Israel from whom the whole twelve tribes sprang. These people were proud Israelites, yet their aspiration for this woman was that she should be like one of their own princesses. It was more than an aspiration; it proved to be prophetic. As we shall see, she was indeed made like Rachel and Leah; she became one of the lineage of Israel's kings and of Israel's Messiah.

God still delights to set beggars among princes, those beggars who have admitted to Him they are beggars. It is the wont of grace to design high and holy privileges and precious spheres of service, and much else, far beyond our expectations, for those who have lain at the foot of the cross as failures and said 'Cover me.' He does far more than just cover us, but says, 'Friend, come up higher;' far higher than we ever asked or thought.

BE FAMOUS, BOAZ!

Then they added a wish specially for Boaz, 'and do thou worthily in Ephratah, and be famous in Bethlehem!' Jesus our Boaz, famous! I love to think of the fame of Jesus, and I ask myself what makes Him famous? Not the number of good Christians He goes around patting on the back saying, 'Well done.' That does not make Him famous, because He can't find any good Christians to pat on the back! He can't pat me on the back and He can't pat you. As God counts good Christians we are all utterly short-weight. What has made Him famous are the sinners He has saved, the failing saints He has restored, the dire situations into which He has brought revival, and the myriad cases in which He has made something beautiful, something good, out of a messed-up life. In the Gospels we have that phrase 'the fame of Jesus' a number of times—'His fame went throughout all Syria,'[1] 'Herod the Tetrarch heard of the fame of Jesus,'[2] and such

---

[1] Matth. 4:24   [2] Matth. 14:1

like. But it was not the wealthy people He had dinner with, or the great ones He consorted with that made Him famous. When sending His message to John the Baptist in prison, He told Him wherein His fame consisted; 'The blind receive their sight, and the lame walk, the lepers are cleansed, and the deaf hear, the dead are raised up, and the poor have the Gospel preached to them.'[1] A pretty motley crew, especially the dead! But it was there that Jesus got His fame. And today He is doing just the same in a moral and spiritual way, and He is justly famous for it. Did you know He gets fame out of meeting your own dire need?

NOT A SECOND BEST

Then the people go on to say, 'And let thy house be like the house of Pharez, whom Tamar bare unto Judah of the seed which the Lord shall give thee of this young woman!' The whole story is given us in Genesis 38, and their point in quoting the case of Tamar was that hers was a similar one to that of Ruth. She had married one of Judah's sons, and he had died leaving her childless. She was another widow in the Old Testament who invoked the law of the *goel*, and one of the family raised up seed by her in her husband's name and Pharez was born. From him came a long and distinguished line, from which, as it happened, Boaz himself had come. Now I suggest they said this because they feared that Boaz and Ruth might feel that, as this was Ruth's second marriage, it was not as good as if she was being married for the first time, that it was a sort of second best. Not at all, they said, this can be as fruitful and important as that of Tamar, from whom the house of Pharez came.

The spiritual application is this. Because some have come to the Lord out of a history of great failure and have done so at a late hour, they may be inclined to think that what they are now receiving from the Lord can only be second best. Let them not believe a word of such a suggestion! Second

[1] Matth. 11:5

best? Second, perhaps, in point of time, but not in quality. Let us agree, you have indeed messed up God's first plan for you; but He has not been defeated; He has an answer to the new situation and has produced a second plan, and who are you to say His second plan is any less good than his first. Note the phrase, second *best*—it is still best, His best for you. Marvellous things have been made of the lives of those who had nothing 'to offer Him but brokenness and strife.' How encouraging it is when someone quotes to us the case of a Tamar, who has been in the same situation as we have and out of whose life has been made 'something beautiful, something good.' Our past or present, whatever it is, need be no barrier to the grace of God.

IN THE LINEAGE OF CHRIST

And so it all came to pass. God did indeed make her life like Rachel and Leah and that house like the house of Pharez. As a result of her union with Boaz, Obed was born, and he in turn became the father of Jesse, and he the father of David, and out of the house and lineage of David according to the flesh Jesus Christ came, the Saviour of the world. And this young Gentile widow, poverty-stricken and without any inheritance, not only had that inheritance restored and herself made the wife of Boaz, but she also took her place in that lineage from whom the Messiah came. And so those aspirations proved to be in reality prophecies.

Now we are given in the last verses of the book of Ruth a little bit of that lineage up to David, but you can see the whole line right up to the Messiah in Matthew 1. Genealogies were always regarded seriously by the Hebrews in the Old Testament and, of course, this one in the New Testament that traces the descent of Jesus Christ on His human side was tremendously important to the Hebrew Christians. It was a documentary evidence which, among many other things, substantiated His claim to be the Messiah, descended from Abraham and David as prophesied. In Hebrew genealogies normally only the father's name is mentioned and there is usually no mention of women in them. But as we cast our eyes down this list before us, we find that four women are named, a deliberate break with convention, and Ruth is one of them. What is of special significance is the fact that each of these women had in the eyes of the world, what we might call a disqualification against them, a sort of black mark.

The first woman mentioned is Tamar, in verse 3: 'and Judah begat Pharez and Zara of Tamar.' I have already said that one of the family played the part of the *goel* and raised up seed for her. What I did not say at that point was that the one who did so was her father-in-law, because her brother-in-law refused to do it. The circumstances in which that took place, all faithfully recorded on the sacred page, are hardly a savoury story and certainly do no credit to any of those involved least of all Tamar. But there she is named in the genealogy of Jesus Christ.

The second woman mentioned is Rahab, in verse 5: 'and Salmon begat Boaz of Rahab.' This was Rahab the prostitute, who hid Joshua's spies just before Jericho was taken. Not only did she save her life by so doing, but was given a place among the Israelites and apparently married one of them, and that one was Salmon, who became the father of Boaz. Yes, Boaz's mother was not only a Gentile, but one who had been a prostitute. Perhaps that was the reason why Boaz had found it difficult to find a bride among the Hebrews.

The third woman mentioned is Ruth, in verse 5: 'and Boaz begat Obed of Ruth.' There was certainly no moral blot against her name, for as Boaz said, 'all the city of my people doth know that thou art a virtuous woman.' But she was a Gentile, normally regarded as an alien from the commonwealth of Israel and a stranger from the covenants of promise.

The fourth woman mentioned is Bathsheba, in verse 6: 'And David the king begat Solomon of her that had been the wife of Uriah.' Well, we all know the shameful story of how she was involved when David in his hour of weakness committed adultery.

What are we to make of the fact that these four women are included in this genealogy? Well, an old commentator on this passage has written somewhere: 'It was to show that sinners might have a share in Christ; for if sinners were among His ancestors, there is a place for sinners among His descendants' —and I'm one of them!

In spite however, of these apparent 'weaknesses' in His human genealogy, His utter Deity and sinlessness remain unaffected, for He was conceived in the womb of Mary not by man but by the Holy Spirit, and declared to be the Son of God with power by His resurrection from the dead. And yet He is the sinner's nearest Kinsman.

A SON FOR NAOMI

Now the last part of our study is this. There was not only a son born for Ruth, but a grandson for Naomi. The book begins with Naomi in her sorrow but ends with Naomi with her lined face wreathed in smiles, holding in her arms a little grandson whom she never expected to see. There are tears on her face, but they are tears of joy. The women her neighbours are as thrilled as she is and they say, 'There is a son (or rather a grandson) born to Naomi.' Actually, by the ties of blood he was not her grandson at all; only Mahlon's son could have been that, but under this gracious law of the *goel* the child born to Boaz and Ruth was accounted her own grandchild, and he was to inherit her son's lands. Her joy knew no bounds as she nursed the little baby in her arms.

Listen further to what these women said, for it has something instructive for us; 'Blessed be the Lord which hath not left thee this day without a kinsman, a *goel*, that his name be famous in Israel.' In other words, whatever losses might occur in her fortunes in the future, there would always be, as this child grew up, a near kinsman to redeem them. 'He shall be unto thee a restorer of thy life, and a nourisher of thine old age.' Never again need she fear the pinch of poverty.

This indicates how we may know a continuation of the experience of grace into which we have entered, or we may put it, how we may know continuous revival. It is only possible as we see the Lord hath not left us without a near Kinsman, Who will be a 'Restorer of our life and a Nourisher of our old age.' Things may go wrong and our spiritual life may begin to ebb, but there at hand is Jesus to restore what may have been lost. And he is ready to do it all the time if you go to Him, for His blood never loses its power. Wherever there has been most ostensibly a continuation of revival in a life or a company of lives, there has always been a continuation of calling sin sin, and a proving of the power of His blood to set free again. He is indeed our nearest Kinsman and the constant Restorer of our life.

And so the story ends with Naomi's face bright with joy, the losses of the past all made good and her future assured.

'Oh,' she says, 'this is a happy, happy ending.'

And so we close the pages of this tender book of Ruth. Ruth passes from our view, so does Boaz, so does Naomi, but the Lord Jesus Christ, our nearest Kinsman, remains to fill our vision.

APPENDIX

Set out below is the text of the book of Ruth as it stands in the Authorised Version (King James Version) together with the text of the two Mosaic laws on which it is based. The text is divided up in such a way that the appropriate portions are put under the chapter headings to which they refer.

REDEMPTION AND REVIVAL IN THE BOOK OF RUTH

Leviticus 25:23–25; 47–49

23. The land shall not be sold for ever; for the land is mine; for ye are strangers and sojourners with me. And in all the land of your possession ye shall grant a redemption for the land. If thy brother be waxen poor, and hath sold away some of his possession, and if any of his kin come to redeem it, then shall he redeem that which his brother sold.

47. And if a sojourner or stranger wax rich by thee, and thy brother that dwelleth by him wax poor, and sell himself unto the stranger or sojourner by thee, or to the stock of the stranger's family: After that he is sold he may be redeemed again; one of his brethren may redeem him: Either his uncle, or his uncle's son, may redeem him, or any that is nigh of kin unto him of his family may redeem him; or if he be able, he may redeem himself.

Deuteronomy 25:5–10

5. If brethren dwell together, and one of them die, and have no child, the wife of the dead shall not marry without unto a stranger: her husband's brother shall go in unto her, and take her to him to wife, and perform the duty of an husband's brother unto her. And it shall be, that the firstborn which she beareth shall succeed in the name of his brother which is dead, that his name be not put out of Israel.

7. And if the man like not to take his brother's wife, then let his brother's wife go up to the gate unto the elders, and say, My husband's brother refuseth to raise up unto his brother a name in Israel, he will not perform the duty of my husband's brother. Then the elders of the city shall call him, and speak unto him: and if he stand to it, and say, I like not to take her; Then shall his brother's wife come unto him in the presence of the elders, and loose his shoe from off his foot, and spit in his face, and shall answer and say, So shall it be done unto that man that will not build up his brother's house. And his name shall be called in Israel, The house of him that hath his shoe loosed.

CHAPTER 2

NAOMI, THE PRODIGAL DAUGHTER OF THE OLD TESTAMENT

Ruth 1:1-22

1. Now it came to pass in the days when the judges ruled, that there was a famine in the land. And a certain man of Bethlehem-Judah went to sojourn in the country of Moab, he, and his wife, and his two sons. And the name of the man was Elimelech, and the name of his wife Naomi, and the name of his two sons Mahlon and Chilion, Ephrathites of Bethlehem-Judah. And they came into the country of Moab and continued there. And Elimelech Noami's husband died; and she was left, and her two sons. And they took them wives of the women of Moab; the name of the one was Orpah, and the name of the other Ruth: and they dwelled there about ten years. And Mahlon and Chilion died also both of them; and the woman was left of her two sons and her husband.

6. Then she arose with her daughters in law, that she might return from the country of Moab: for she had heard in the country of Moab how that the Lord had visited his people in giving them bread. Wherefore she went forth out of the place where she was, and her two daughters in law with her; and they went on the way to return unto the land of Judah. And Naomi said unto her two daughters in law, Go, return each to her mother's house: the Lord deal kindly with you, as ye have dealt with the dead, and with me. The Lord grant you that ye may find rest, each of you in the house of her husband. Then she kissed them; and they lifted up their voice and wept. And they said unto her, Surely we will return with thee

unto thy people. And Naomi said, Turn again, my daughters: why will ye go with me? are there yet any more sons in my womb, that they may be your husbands? Turn again, my daughters, go your way; for I am too old to have an husband. If I should say, I have hope, if I should have an husband also to night, and should also bear sons; Would ye tarry for them till they were grown? Would ye stay for them from having husbands? nay, my daughters; for it grieveth me much for your sakes that the hand of the Lord is gone out against me. And they lifted up their voice, and wept again: and Orpah kissed her mother in law; but Ruth clave unto her.

15. And she said, Behold, thy sister in law is gone back unto her people, and unto her gods: return thou after thy sister in law. And Ruth said, Intreat me not to leave thee, or to return from following after thee: for whither thou goest, I will go; and where thou lodgest, I will lodge: thy people shall be my people, and thy God my God: Where thou diest, will I die, and there will I be buried: the Lord do so to me, and more also, if ought but death part thee and me. When she saw that she was steadfastly minded to go with her, then she left speaking unto her.

19. So they two went until they came to Bethlehem. And it came to pass, when they were come to Bethlehem, that all the city was moved about them, and they said, Is this Naomi? And she said unto them, Call me not Naomi, call me Mara: for the Almighty hath dealt very bitterly with me. I went out full, and the Lord hath brought me home again empty: why then call ye me Naomi, seeing the Lord hath testified against me, and the Almighty hath afflicted me? So Naomi returned, and Ruth the Moabitess, her daughter in law, with her, which returned out of the country of Moab: and they came to Bethlehem in the beginning of barley harvest.

CHAPTER 3

BOAZ, THE NEAR KINSMAN

Ruth 2:1, 20

1. And Naomi had a kinsman of her husband's, a mighty man of wealth, *of* the family of Elimelech; and his name was Boaz.

20. And Naomi said unto her daughter in law, Blessed be he of the Lord, who hath not left off his kindness to the living and to the dead. And Naomi said unto her, The man is near of kin unto us, one of our next kinsmen.

CHAPTER 4

RUTH, A GLEANER IN THE FIELD OF BOAZ

Ruth 2:1–23

1. And Naomi had a kinsman of her husband's, a mighty man of wealth, of the family of Elimelech; and his name was Boaz. And Ruth the Moabitess said unto Naomi, Let me now go to the field, and glean ears of corn after him in whose sight I shall find grace. And she said unto her, Go, my daughter. And she went, and came, and gleaned in the field after the reapers: and her hap was to light on a part of the field belonging unto Boaz, who was of the kindred of Elimelech. And, behold, Boaz came from Bethlehem, and said unto the reapers, The Lord be with you. And they answered him, The Lord bless thee. Then said Boaz unto his servant that was set over the reapers, Whose damsel is this? And the servant that was set over the reapers answered and said, It is the Moabitish damsel that came back with Naomi out of the country of Moab: And she said, I pray you, let me glean and gather after the reapers among the sheaves: so she came, and hath continued even from the morning until now, that she tarried a little in the house.

8. Then said Boaz unto Ruth, Hearest thou not, my daughter? Go not to glean in another field, neither go from hence, but abide here fast by my maidens: Let thine eyes be on the field that they do reap, and go thou after them: have I not charged the young men that they shall not touch thee? and when thou art athirst, go unto the vessels, and drink of that which the young men have drawn. Then she fell on her face, and bowed herself to the ground, and said unto him, Why have I found grace in thine eyes, that thou shouldest take knowledge of me, seeing I am a stranger? And Boaz answered and said unto her, It hath fully been shewed me, all that thou hast done unto thy mother in law since the death of thine husband: and how thou hast left thy father and thy mother, and the land of thy nativity, and art come unto a people which thou knewest not heretofore. The Lord recompense thy work, and a full reward be given thee of the Lord God of Israel, under whose wings thou art come to trust. Then she said, Let me find favour in thy sight, my Lord; for that thou hast comforted me, and for that thou hast spoken friendly unto thine handmaid, though I be not like unto one of thine handmaidens. And Boaz said unto her, At mealtime come thou hither, and eat of the bread, and dip thy morsel in the vinegar. And she sat beside the reapers: and he reached her parched corn, and she did eat and was sufficed, and left. And when she was risen up to glean, Boaz

commanded his young men, saying, Let her glean even among the sheaves, and reproach her not: and let fall also some of the handfuls of purpose for her, and leave them, that she may glean them, and rebuke her not. So she gleaned in the field until even, and beat out that she had gleaned: and it was about an ephah of barley.

18. And she took it up, and went into the city: and her mother in law saw what she had gleaned: and she brought forth, and gave to her that she had reserved after she was sufficed. And her mother in law said unto her, Where hast thou gleaned to day? and where wroughtest thou? blessed be he that did take knowledge of thee. And she shewed her mother in law with whom she had wrought, and said, The man's name with whom I wrought to day is Boaz. And Naomi said unto her daughter in law, Blessed be he of the Lord, who hath not left off his kindness to the living and to the dead. And Naomi said unto her, The man is near of kin unto us, one of our next kinsman. And Ruth the Moabitess said, He said unto me also, Thou shalt keep fast by my young men, until they have ended all my harvest. And Naomi said unto Ruth her daughter in law, It is good, my daughter, that thou go out with his maidens, that they meet thee not in any other field. So she kept fast by the maidens of Boaz to glean unto the end of barley harvest and of wheat harvest; and dwelt with her mother in law.

CHAPTER 5

RUTH AT THE FEET OF BOAZ

Ruth 3:1–18

1. Then Naomi her mother in law said unto her, My daughter, shall I not seek rest for thee, that it may be well with thee? And now is not Boaz of our kindred, with whose maidens thou wast? Behold, he winnoweth barley to night in the threshingfloor. Wash thyself therefore, and anoint thee, and put thy raiment upon thee, and get thee down to the floor: but make not thyself known unto the man, until he shall have done eating and drinking. And it shall be, when he lieth down, that thou shalt mark the place where he shall lie, and thou shalt go in, and uncover his feet, and lay thee down; and he will tell thee what thou shalt do. And she said unto her, All that thou sayest unto me I will do.

6. And she went down unto the floor, and did according to all that her mother in law bade her, and when Boaz had eaten and drunk, and his heart was merry, he went to lie down at the end of the heap

of corn: and she came softly, and uncovered his feet, and laid her down.

8. And it came to pass at midnight, that the man was afraid, and turned himself: and, behold, a woman lay at his feet. And he said, Who art thou? And she answered, I am Ruth thine handmaid: spread therefore thy skirt over thine handmaid; for thou art a near kinsman. And he said, Blessed be thou of the Lord, my daughter: for thou hast shewed more kindness in the latter end than at the beginning, inasmuch as thou followedst not young men, whether poor or rich. And now, my daughter, fear not; I will do to thee all that thou requirest: for all the city of my people doth know that thou art a virtuous woman. And now it is true that I am thy near kinsman: howbeit there is a kinsman nearer than I. Tarry this night, and it shall be in the morning, that if he will perform unto thee the part of a kinsman, well; let him do the kinsman's part: but if he will not do the part of a kinsman to thee, then will I do the part of a kinsman to thee, as the Lord liveth: lie down until the morning.

14. And she lay at his feet until the morning: and she rose up before one could know another. And he said, Let it not be known that a woman came into the floor, Also he said, Bring the vail that thou hast upon thee, and hold it. And when she held it, he measured six measures of barley, and laid it on her: and she went into the city. And when she came to her mother in law, she said, Who art thou, my daughter? And she told her all that the man had done to her. And she said, These six measures of barley gave he me; for he said to me, Go not empty unto thy mother in law. Then said she, Sit still, my daughter, until thou know how the matter will fall: for the man will not be in rest, until he have finished the thing this day.

CHAPTER 6

BOAZ AND THE NEARER KINSMAN

Ruth 4:1–8

1. Then went Boaz up to the gate, and sat him down there: and, behold, the kinsman of whom Boaz spake came by; unto whom he said, Ho, such a one! turn aside, sit down here. And he turned aside, and sat down. And he took ten men of the elders of the city, and said, Sit ye down here. And they sat down. And he said unto the kinsman, Naomi, that is come again out of the country of Moab, selleth a parcel of land, which was our brother Elimelech's: And I thought to advertise thee, saying, Buy it before the inhabitants, and before the elders of my people. If thou wilt redeem it, redeem it: but

if thou wilt not redeem it, then tell me, that I may know: for there is none to redeem it beside thee; and I am after thee. And he said, I will redeem it. Then said Boaz, What day thou buyest the field of the hand of Naomi, thou must buy it also of Ruth the Moabitess, the wife of the dead, to raise up the name of the dead upon his inheritance.

6. And the kinsman said, I cannot redeem it for myself, lest I mar mine own inheritance: redeem thou my right to thyself; for I cannot redeem it. Now this was the manner in former time in Israel concerning redeeming and concerning changing, for to confirm all things; a man plucked off his shoe and gave it to his neighbour; and this was a testimony in Israel. Therefore the kinsman said unto Boaz, Buy it for thee. So he drew off his shoe.

CHAPTER 7

THE HAPPY ENDING

Ruth 4:9–22

9. And Boaz said unto the elders, and unto all the people, Ye are witnesses this day, that I have bought all that was Elimelech's, and all that was Chilion's: and Mahlon's, of the hand of Naomi. Moreover Ruth the Moabitess, the wife of Mahlon, have I purchased to be my wife, to raise up the name of the dead upon his inheritance, that the name of the dead be not cut off from among his brethren, and from the gate of his place: ye are witnesses this day. And all the people that were in the gate, and the elders, said, we are witnesses. The Lord make the woman that is come into thine house like Rachel and like Leah, which two did build the house of Israel: and do thou worthily in Ephratah, and be famous in Bethlehem: and let thy house be like the house of Pharez, whom Tamar bare unto Judah, of the seed which the Lord shall give thee of this young woman.

13. So Boaz took Ruth, and she was his wife: and when he went in unto her, the Lord gave her conception, and she bare a son. And the women said unto Naomi, Blessed be the Lord, which hath not left thee this day without a kinsman, that his name may be famous in Israel. And he shall be unto thee a restorer of thy life, and a nourisher of thine old age: for thy daughter in law, which loveth thee, which is better to thee than seven sons, hath born him. And Naomi took the child, and laid it in her bosom, and became nurse unto it. And the women her neighbours gave it a name, saying,

There is a son born to Naomi; and they called his name Obed: he is the father of Jesse, the father of David.

18. Now these are the generations of Pharez: Pharez begat Hezron, And Hezron begat Ram, and Ram begat Amminadab, And Amminadab begat Nahshon, and Nahshon begat Salmon, And Salmon begat Boaz, and Boaz begat Obed, and Obed begat Jesse, and Jesse begat David.